CIVIL WAR

PERIOD

COOKERY

A Unique Collection of Favorite Recipes from Notable People & Families Involved in the War Between the States

Robert W. Pelton

Copyright © 2003 by Robert W. Pelton

ISBN 0-7414-0971-2

Published by:

INFINITY
PUBLISHING.COM

Infinity Publishing.com
519 West Lancaster Avenue
Haverford, PA 19041-1413
Info@buybooksontheweb.com
www.buybooksontheweb.com
Toll-free (877) BUY BOOK
Local Phone (610) 520-2500
Fax (610) 519-0261

Printed in the United States of America

Printed on Recycled Paper

Published April, 2003

COVERS SUCH CATEGORIES AS:

Confederate Military Leaders
Union Military leaders
Political Leaders of the Period
Heroes of the Blue and the Gray
Famous Women of the Civil War Era
Men of the Times Who Gained
   a Measure of Fame

INCLUDES THE FAVORITE RECIPES OF:

General Robert E. Lee
Abner Doubleday
Henry Ward Beecher
General Ulysses S. Grant
Abraham Lincoln
Captain John Mosby
Horace Greeley
Nathan Bedford Forrest
General William Sherman
Jefferson Davis
George Armstrong Custer
Stonewall Jackson

Part of the Pelton Historical
                    Cookbook Series.

Includes the Following Titles:

   Historical Thanksgiving Cookery

   Revolutionary War Period Cookery

   Historical Christmas Cookery

Dedication

To Barnabus Horton of Leichestershire, England, a Puritan, who bravely sailed to the Colonies on the *Swallow* some time between 1633 and 1638. He was accompanied by his wife and two sons, Joseph and Benjamin. The family landed at Hampton, Massachusetts.

And to my Great-great grandmother Huldah Radike Horton, one of the finest and most famous horsewomen of her day. She had the honor of entertaining Lafayette in her home and riding along side him in a parade held in his honor in Newburg, New York, in 1824. The French General and friend of our young Republic was making his second and last visit.

Contents

Preface

Civil War Period Cookery

Civil War Period Cookery is chock full of delightfully delicious cooking ideas favored by many famous people of days long past. It contains the prized recipes for those dishes cooked by, or eaten by, some of the better known as well as lesser-known figures from the Civil War era of our glorious history. Included are recipes for tasty breads and interesting baked goods, skillet southern fried chicken and really good poultry dishes. Here you will also be treated to many taste-tempting soups, stews and stuffings – and, yes, even pickles as well as loads of other wonderful things. Or you may wish to try some buttermilk pie, an array of wonderful desserts, rhubarb punch and other delightful beverages. Then make the unique corn bread with a streak of delicious custard running through it. Yes, you can now enjoy a meal exactly like that eaten by those who wore both the blue and the gray during the War Between the States – or as some unreconstructed Southerners still refer to it – the War of Northern Aggression.

Here you will find the favorites of such historical luminaries as Gilbert van Camp who dearly loved sweet potato biscuits for breakfast. Or those honey cookies eaten by President Abraham Lincoln. And the special pork and parsnip stew so enjoyed by Medal of Honor winner, Dr.

Mary Edwards Walker. That unusual molasses pie made by the wife of famed Confederate Colonel Nathan Bedford Forrest. Or those special huckleberry pancakes so dearly loved by General Robert E. Lee. And the giblet-cornmeal turkey stuffing prepared on special holidays by the Abner Doubleday family

One very special traditional cake recipe handed down from the Civil War era is this favorite from the family of Confederate Brigadier General Roger Atkinson Pryor (1828-1919). Mrs. Pryor made this wonderful sponge cake for her family each Christmas season in three distinct steps as follows:

SPONGE CAKE

Step 1:

5 egg whites	5 egg yolks
1 cup sugar, sifted 4 times	½ lemon, rind only (grated)
1 tbls lemon juice	1 cup flour, sifted 4 times
	¼ tsp salt

Beat egg whites until stiff. Gradually beat in 5 tbls of the sugar and set aside. Add lemon juice to egg yolks and beat until lemon colored and so thick that beater turns with difficulty. Add grated lemon rind and beat in remaining sugar. Combine egg yolks with egg whites and fold together with a spoon until mixture is blended evenly, Mix and sift together flour and salt in separate bowl. Fold this into egg mixture. Do not beat after adding flour to avoid breaking air bubbles. Pour into an unbuttered 9-inch tube pan. Cut through mixture several times to break air bubbles. Bake at 350 degrees for 1 hour or more. When cake is done, loosen with spatula or knife and remove from tube pan. Turn out on wire rack and let stand until cool.

CUSTARD

Step 2:

4 cups milk	½ cup sugar
2 eggs, beaten slightly	¼ tsp salt
	1 tsp vanilla extract

Scald milk in covered saucepan. In a separate saucepan, combine beaten eggs with sugar and salt. Blend well. Stir scalded milk into egg mixture and stir constantly. Let cook until mixture coats spoon. Set aside and chill. Then stir in vanilla. If custard should curdle, beat until smooth.

CAKE ASSEMBLY

Step 3:

3 cups split almonds, blanched   1-1/2 cups sherry wine
½ pint heavy cream

Carefully slice cake into three layers. Stick 1 cup of split almonds into each layer, dividing them as evenly as possible. Pour 1/2 cup of the sherry wine over each layer as it is reassembled. An hour before serving, pour the soft custard over the cake. Make occasional deep gashes with a knife so custard will seep all the way through cake. Whip the cream and place on cake in large tablespoonfuls.

General Roger Atkinson Pryor was an influential Christian newspaper publisher in Virginia and a firebrand secessionist. He resigned from his first term in Congress in 1861 to join the Confederate Army and fought heroically at Seven Pines and Williamsburg. An impatient man who was disillusioned with the political machinations of the Confederate War Department, he resigned his commission and went on to fight as a mere private in August of 1863 with General Fitzhugh Lee's cavalry brigade. Pryor was taken prisoner by Union troops near Petersburg in November of 1864, but was given his freedom in a prisoner exchange a few months later.

To sum everything up, each recipe found in this unique cook book was once popular, or at least commonly used during the Civil War period. They were all part of the history of a particular family, or person, who lived and loved and prayed and fought through this tragic time of our great nation. Many were coveted treasures within a family, some famous, some not so famous, and handed down through the years or lost with the passage of time. Each recipe has been meticulously updated. When the recipe is used today, it will turn out exactly as it did for the woman of the house that prepared it for her family so many long years ago. Here they are presented for the first time for today's American families to enjoy and experience the pleasure of preparing, cooking, baking and serving – exactly as it was done in the past. And lastly, to thankfully pass a blessing over before eating – be it for breakfast, lunch or dinner.

.

Introducing Civil War Period Cookery

Some of the recipes used during the Civil War era, as originally written, would be rather difficult, if not in some cases nearly impossible, to use with any degree of accuracy or ease. This can readily be attested to by this Chestnut family "Recipe" for BILLY GOAT COOKIES as given below. This one was simple written down as a list of ingredients by Mrs. Chestnut. In such cases, the homemaker was expected to know exactly what to do in order to achieve the desired end result. Here it is as originally inscribed in the Chestnut family ledger:

3 Cups Flour	*1 Cup Raisins Chopped Fine*
1 Cup Butter	*1 Cup Walnuts Chopped Fine*
1 ½ Cups Brown Sugar	*1 Teaspoon Soda (scant)*
3 Eggs	*sifted in Flour*
	¼ Cup Water (Scant)

Brigadier General James Chestnut, Jr (1815-1885) was a fiery orator, an ardent secessionist and a staunch defender of slavery. This fourth generation South Carolina planter was a Princeton graduate and a devout Christian. He was an aide-de-camp to General P.G.T. Beauregard at Fort Sumter and First Bull Run. Chestnut was later a most trusted adviser to President of the Confederacy, Jefferson Davis, as well as his aide-de-camp from 1862 to 1864.

On the other hand, a great many other recipes were simply given as one long and often rather complicated paragraph. Ingredients weren't usually listed in any particular order. This recipe for BAKED CAULIFLOWER is a good example of how they were once commonly written. It was a favorite of the Garfield family:

"One and one-half pounds cauliflower, 2 ounces butter, 1 gill milk, 1 dessertspoonful meat extract, 2 tablespoons flour, a dash of ground mace. Boil the cauliflower; heat 1-1/2 ounces butter and 2 tablespoons flour to a golden brown; add the milk and a tumblerful of water in which the cauliflower has been boiled with 2 saltspoonfuls meat extract dissolved in it; boil this sauce till thick, then flavor with ground mace; strain and pour over the cauliflower, which has been placed in a deep dish; melt the remaining ½ ounce butter, pour it over, sprinkle with grated cheddar cheese and bake in a hot oven, standing the dish in a pan of boiling water."

James Abram Garfield (1831-1881) pulled himself up by his bootstraps from a poor childhood and became a lay preacher, later a Union General during the War Between the States and finally the President of the United States. This remarkable Christian individualist led brigades at Shiloh, Middle Creek and Pound Gap and was General William Rosecrans Chief of Staff in the Chickamauga Campaign.

Here is a most interesting old recipe for OX-TAIL SOUP as it was prepared for and often enjoyed by George Armstrong Custer (1839-76) who is most often remembered in history as an Indian fighter against the Cheyennes. This young man gained lasting fame with what became known as

"Custer's Last Stand" when he and his army was meticulously slaughtered by Sitting Bull's warriors at Little Big Horn on June 23, 1876. Here is the Custer family original recipe:

"One ox tail, 2 pounds lean beef, 4 carrots, 3 onions, parsley, thyme, pepper and salt to taste, 4 quarts cold water. Cut tail into joints, fry brown in good drippings. Slice onions and 2 carrots and fry in the same when you have taken out all of the pieces of tail. When done tie the thyme and parsley in lace bag and drop into the soup pot. Put in the tail, then the beef cut into strips. Grate over them 2 whole carrots. Pour over all the water and boil slowly 4 hours. Strain and season. Thicken with brown flour wet with cold water. Boil 15 minutes longer and serve."

Few People realize that Custer was only 37 when he died. This tall handsome Bible believing cavalryman, with his famed curly blonde flowing locks, was unbelievably courageous. He was an 1861 West Point graduate who saw much action as a Union officer during the Civil War. Custer fought heroically at such places as Gettysburg, Appomattox,

Bull Run, Winchester, Cedar Creek, Richmond and Five Forks. More than 10,000 Confederate prisoners were captured under his command alone!

Measurements for ingredients used in recipes used in the past would not be recognizable to more modern homemakers. Look at some of those called for in the recipes given above – 1 gill of milk; 1 dessertspoonful meat extract; a tumblerful of water; a dash of ground mace; 1 saltspoonful. What exactly would they mean today? Or for example, when busily scurrying around the kitchen and preparing a meal, who would be able to properly measure ingredients in such things as a wineglassful? Or a pound of milk or water? Then try a dram of liquid? What about a pound of eggs?

Here is a list of a few of the more unusual measurements sometimes used by housewives and others during the Civil War period. The original is first given followed by its modern day counterpart:

Pound of eggs	9 large eggs
	12 medium eggs
Pound of solid fat	1 pint
Pound of milk	1 pint
Saltspoonful	¼ teaspoon
Dessertspoonful	2 teaspoons
Wineglassful	4 tablespoons
Tumblerful	½ pint
Teacupful	¾ cup
Coffecupful	1 cup
Kitchencupful	1 cup
1 gill	½ cup
Dash pepper	1/8 teaspoon
1 fluid dram	1 teaspoon

Horace Greeley (1811-72), the famed *New York Tribune* journalist was a Christian as can be attested to by his own words: ***"It is impossible to mentally or socially enslave a***

Bible-reading people. The principles of the Bible are the groundwork of human freedom. ... 'Perfect through suffering' was the way traced out by the Great Captain of our Salvation." One of Greeley's favorite breakfast dishes was this OMELET SOUFFLE as prepared for him often in his home:

> *"Take three eggs, two ounces of butter, one dessertspoon of chopped parsley, one saltspoon of chopped onions and one pinch of dried herbs. Beat the whites of the eggs to a very stiff froth. Mix the yolks with the parsley and a little salt and pepper. Stir the herbs gently into them and continue as in a plain omelet. Fold the omelet and serve immediately."*

The words of Mr. Greeley regarding the right of the various states to secede from the Union are still well worth considering. Our history books make no mention of them, perhaps for very good reason. They did not make him very popular in his day with his Northern counterparts, and in fact they brought the wrath of many down on his head. He stated it this way: *"The right to secede may be a revolting one, but it exists nevertheless. ... We hope never to live in a Republic where one section is pinned to the other section by bayonets. If the Declaration of Independence justified the secession of 3,000,000 colonists in 1776, I do not see why the Constitution ratified by the same men would not justify the secession of 5,000,000 Southerners from the Federal Union in 1861."*

However we label it, the consequences of the monstrous War Between the States shattered our fragile Republic as nothing ever did before it or since. The Union military machine was the victorious invader of the South. And its Radical Republican, hate-filled Northern politicians were vengeful punishers of their defeated Southern brothers and sisters. The terrible deeds inflicted upon the South by their Northern brothers were uncalled for as history has clearly shown us. And as time has proven – unforgiven, by and large, by the Southern people.

President Abraham Lincoln did not intend for this to happen, nor after his assassination, did his successor, President Andrew Johnson. A Radical Republican Congress overrode his Presidential veto and rammed through the infamous *Reconstruction Act of 1867* against his wishes. Yet fanatics such as Secretary of War Edwin M. Stanton and ferocious orator Thaddeus Stevens, a founder and leader of the Radical Republicans, were determined to severely punish the defeated South and its leaders. Stevens was instrumental in bringing impeachment charges of "high crimes and misdemeanors" against Johnson who was subsequently acquitted by only a single vote in May of 1868.

The editors of *Harper's Weekly* were out for blood. They arrogantly spewed out their venom against the South and its leadership. In one instance it had the audacity to demand: ***"Jefferson Davis must be tried for treason. If convicted he must be sentenced. If sentenced he must be hanged."*** Yes, this was typically the only kind of retribution acceptable to some fanatics in the North – to violently take the life of one of the greatest Christian leaders on either side of the War. Fortunately, more stable minded people disagreed and were able to stop such extreme actions. Yet, this most admirable Southern gentleman, a graduate of West Point, was still inhumanely imprisoned for 2 years at Fortress Monroe while never having been brought to trial. And while in prison, he was allowed only to have his *Bible* and his Episcopal prayer book to read.

1

Griddle Cakes, Pancakes and Waffles the Old Fashioned Way

Sour Milk Corn Meal Pancakes from the Hampton Family

1 cup corn meal	1 tsp salt
1 cup flour	2 cups sour milk
½ tsp baking powder	2 cups sour cream
1-1/4 tsp baking soda	1 egg, well beaten

Sift together the corn meal, flour baking powder, baking soda and salt in a wooden mixing bowl. Beat in the sour milk, sour cream and the beaten egg. Drop by spoonfuls on hot griddle. Cook until lightly browned on both sides. This recipe makes 16 servings.

** ** ** ** **

Confederate General Wade Hampton (1818-1902 was wounded during the first battle of Bull Run but recovered in time to heroically lead an infantry brigade during the Peninsular Campaign in the Spring of 1862. A fearless warrior, Hampton was known to always have his *Bible* at his side when riding into battle. He was later wounded three more times at Gettysburg. Hamptom was one of the wealthiest planters in South Carolina before the war, having been born into an aristocratic Christian family. He fought with J.E.B. Stuart's cavalry corps and rose to become second in command. When Stuart was killed in May of 1864, Hampton was given command of Robert E. Lee's cavalry corps. When the Civil War finally ended, General Hampton went back to his South Carolina estate and made an effort to rebuild his now shrunken fortune. He got involved politically in an effort to thwart the horrendous Radical Republican Reconstruction policies construed by hate-filled Northern politicians to punish the South and its leaders. Hampton was elected Governor in 1876 (defeating a "carpetbagger" incumbent), re-elected in 1878, and then went on to the Senate a short time later.

The Beauregard Family's Buckwheat Griddle Cakes

½ yeast cake	1-1/2 tsp salt
4 cups lukewarm water	Buckwheat flour to suit
1 tbls brown sugar	¼ tsp baking soda

Soften the yeast in 1 cup of the lukewarm warm water. Put into a mixing bowl and stir in the brown sugar (or molasses may be substituted), salt, the other 3 cups of lukewarm water and enough buckwheat flour to make a thin batter. Cover with a towel and set aside to rise overnight in a warm place. In the morning, add the baking soda which has been dissolved in 1 tablespoon of cold water. Beat thoroughly and drop by tablespoonfuls on hot griddle. Cook until nicely browned on both sides.

** ** ** ** **

Pierre Gustave Toutant Beauregard (1818-93) was a famed Confederate General during the Civil War. Born into a wealthy Louisiana Creole family, he graduated second in his class at West Point in 1838. Beauregard, a professed Christian, became the new Confederacy's first hero with his successful military assault on Fort Sumter. He always went by the name of P.G.T. Beauregard which is quite understandable with all of those unique and sometimes difficult to pronounce names. Beauregard saw much action at such places as Charleston, Battle of First Manassas, Bull Run, Shiloh, and Petersburg. Highly thought of as a military tactician and leader, he rejected numerous offers of senior command positions in the Egyptian Army after the Civil War ended. He instead returned to Louisiana and ran the New Orleans, Jackson & Mississippi Railway for a period of five years, was in charge of the Louisiana Lottery, and in 1888 became the Commissioner of Public Works in New Orleans.

The Evart's Family Plain White Potato Pancakes

1 cup mashed potatoes	2 tbls sugar
2 cups milk	1-1/2 tbls baking powder
2 eggs, well beaten	1-1/2 cups flour
2 tsp salt	3 tbls fat, melted

Put the mashed potatoes in a wooden mixing bowl. Blend in the milk, frothy beaten eggs, salt and sugar. Sift together the baking powder and flour. Stir this into the mixture in the bowl. Lastly blend in the melted fat. Beat thoroughly to a creamy batter. Drop by spoonfuls into a hot, well-greased cast iron skillet. Turn over once so pancakes are lightly browned on both sides. Serve while hot with butter and maple syrup or sugar sprinkled over the top.

** ** ** ** **

William Maxwell Evarts (1818-1901) of Boston was a widely known New York attorney who not only possessed a great legal mind but was also an unsurpassed orator. At the conclusion of the Civil War he was selected to serve as a member of the legal team hired by the government to prosecute former Confederate President Jefferson Davis. Prior to this, Evarts was sent to England by the Union government in 1863 and 1864. His task was an important one – he was to use his influence to forcibly persuade the British to stop building and equipping ships for the Confederate Navy. Evarts, a church going Christian, was also a member of the high powered legal team President Andrew Johnson used to defend him during his impeachment trial. Evarts alone, because of his phenomenal legal skills, is given credit for keeping Johnson from being impeached and thrown out of office. Johnson duly rewarded him with an appointment as Attorney General of the United States from 1867-1868. And he served as Secretary of State under President Rutherford Hayes from 1877 to 1881.

Kentucky Waffles – A Lomax Breakfast Favorite

3 egg yolks, well beaten 1 cup milk
2 pints flour, sifted   2 tbls lard, melted
1 pint sour cream   1 tsp baking soda
                3 egg whites, well beaten

Combine the beaten egg yolks, sifted flour and sour cream in a wooden mixing bowl and blend together. Make batter thin by adding the milk. Then stir in melted lard. Dissolve baking soda in a little cold milk and stir this into the mixture in bowl. Lastly fold in beaten egg whites. Bake quickly in hot waffle iron. Serve while steaming hot with butter and maple syrup.

** ** ** ** **

General Lunsford Lindsay Lomax (1835-1913) was born in Rhode Island, graduated from West Point, and then spent time gaining military experience on the Western frontier as an Indian fighter. Since his father was already an army officer from Virginia when the Civil War started, Lomax applied for and was given a commission as a captain in the Confederate Army. This young man, raised in a God fearing Christian family, was soon after appointed assistant adjutant general to General Joseph E. Johnston. Lomax distinguished himself under fire at Petersburg, Gettysburg and the Wilderness Campaign. He was captured by Union forces at Woodstock but was able to escape. He, along with General Johnston, later surrendered after the Carolinas Campaign.

Rice Waffles – A Sheridan Family Favorite

1-1/2 cups flour	1 cup milk
1 tbls baking powder	2 egg yolks
¼ tsp salt	2 tbls butter, melted
2 tbls sugar	1 cup rice, boiled
2 egg whites, stiffly beaten	

Sift together in a wooden mixing bowl the flour, baking powder, salt and sugar. Stir in the milk, egg yolks, melted butter and rice. Blend everything thoroughly. Lastly, fold in the stiffly beaten egg whites. Place batter in a pitcher and pour correct amount onto a hot, well-greased waffle iron. Close top and cook until well done. Serve while hot with butter and syrup. Makes 4 large waffles.

** ** ** ** **

Union General Philip Henry Sheridan (1831-88), barely five feet tall, was the son of Irish immigrants. He graduated from West Point with the class of 1853 after having been suspended for a year because he had threatened another cadet with a bayonet. This pugnacious, short-tempered man was looked upon by many Northerners as a hero during the Civil War. His troops defeated Robert E. Lee decisively on April 1, 1865, at Five Forks, Virginia. And he again thrashed Lee's Confederate forces on April 6, 1865, at Sailor's Creek. Sheridan destroyed everything in his path as he ferociously led his troops into battle after battle. In one instance, he went on a ruthless rampage, reporting to General Grant that he had burned 2,000 barns and 700 mills. This squat little bully was despised throughout Texas and Louisiana where he served as the postwar military governor. President Andrew Johnson had to order his recall because of the dictatorial manner in which he rigorously enforced Reconstruction policies.

Velvet Huckleberry Pancakes – One of Robert E. Lee's Favorites

2-1/2 cups flour	2 cups milk
4 tsp baking powder	2 egg yolks, beaten
½ tsp salt	1 tbls butter, melted
1-1/2 tbls sugar	2 cups huckleberries

2 egg whites, stiffly beaten

Sift together in a wooden mixing bowl the flour, baking powder, salt and sugar. Combine the milk, beaten egg yolks and melted butter in a separate bowl and blend thoroughly. Add this mixture slowly to the dry ingredients in first bowl. Beat until smooth. Stir in the huckleberries. Lastly, fold in stiffly beaten egg whites. Drop by large mixing spoonfuls on hot greased griddle. When bubbles appear and it starts to brown around edges, flip pancake over and cook on other side. Serve while hot and spread thickly with butter and honey as General Lee did. He also enjoyed eating them with maple syrup generously poured over the butter.

** ** ** ** **

General Robert E. Lee (1807-70) was the third son of Revolutionary War hero Light Horse Harry Lee. He graduated second in his class at West Point in 1828 and went on to become the Confederacy's greatest battlefield commander. By the time the Civil War broke out, Lee was considered by his colleagues and his superiors to be the U.S. Army's most promising officer. Lincoln offered him field command of the Union Army but he instead resigned his commission when Virginia left the Union. Robert E. Lee became a legend and rightfully so. He ranks among the world's greatest military leaders and was what Americans still point to with pride as the ideal gentleman Christian soldier. Lee had this to say regarding the Bible: ***"There are things in the old Book which I may not be able to explain, but I fully accept it as the infallible Word of God, and receive its teachings as inspired by the Holy Spirit."***

The McCormick Family Rolled Oats Buttermilk Pancakes

2 cups rolled oats	1 tbls sugar
2-1/2 cups buttermilk	1 tsp salt
1-1/2 cups flour	2 tbls butter, melted
1 tsp baking powder	2 tbls water
1 tsp baking soda	1 tsp maple syrup
2 eggs, slightly beaten	

Put the rolled oats and buttermilk in a wooden mixing bowl and let soak 10 minutes. Then sift into this the flour, baking powder, baking soda, sugar, and salt. Blend everything together well. Stir in the melted butter, water, maple syrup and beaten eggs. Beat thoroughly. Drop by tablespoonfuls on hot greased griddle. Brown lightly on both sides. Serve while hot with butter and syrup. Makes 24 servings.

** ** ** ** **

Cyrus Hall McCormick (1809-84) was one of America's greatest inventors of harvesting machinery. So important was his reaper to the outcome of the Civil War that Secretary of War Edwin Stanton said this: *"Without McCormick's invention, I feel the North could not win and that the Union would be dismembered."* McCormick was a man who had been brought up in a solid Christian family. He credited his genius to God and said that *"the Lord always gives a person the talents he possesses, and allows a person to either use or not to use those talents. I personally choose to always try and follow the Lord's will in my life."*

2

Soups and Salads to Not be Forgotten

Mashed Potato Soup – A Farragut Family Dinner Specialty

4 cups milk	1 tbls flour
2 tbls onion, grated	1-1/2 tsp salt
2 cups mashed potatoes	Pinch pepper
3 tbls butter, melted	¼ tsp celery flakes

1 tbls parsley, chopped fine

Scald the milk and grated onion together in a large soup pot. Slowly stir in the mashed potatoes. Blend half the melted butter with the flour, salt, pepper and celery flakes in a cup. Add this to the soup mixture and blend well. Bring to a boil and let boil I minute. Take off stove, add the rest of the butter and sprinkle over top with chopped parsley.

** ** ** ** **

David Glascow Farragut (1801-70), a Tennessean by birth, but orphaned at an early age, was given his first ship command when he was but 12 years old. He later had the distinction of becoming the first Admiral in the United States Navy. This honor was bestowed upon him during the Civil War. On August 5, 1864, this man destroyed the Confederate fleet in Mobile Bay. He is best remembered in history for his famous declaration when under fire: *"Damn the torpedoes – full steam ahead!"* He was a true American hero in every sense of the word. Admiral Farragut was a devout, Bible believing Christian man. His son. Loyall wrote that his father had once told him: *"He never felt so near his Master as he did when in a storm, knowing that on his skill depended the safety of so many lives."*

Bean Soup as Made by Mrs. Hamlin

1 cup beans, dried	1 tsp pepper
1 small onion, sliced thin	3 cups milk
3 slices bacon, diced	1 tbls butter
3 tsp salt	1 cup tomatoes, cooked

Put beans in pot of water and let soak overnight. Drain in the morning and cover with 6 cups fresh water. Add sliced onion and diced bacon pieces. Cover pot and cook for several hours or until beans are tender. Stir in 2 teaspoons salt and ½ teaspoon pepper near end of cooking time. When tender, press beans through a sieve. Stir in milk and butter. Heat while stirring constantly. Lastly add cooked tomatoes and the rest of salt and pepper. Continue stirring until thoroughly heated. Serve immediately with corn bread.

** ** ** ** **

Hannibal Hamlin (1809-91), a lawyer from Maine, is a man few people remember in American history. He has been lost and forgotten with the passage of time. But this professed Christian did experience his day of greatness. He was President Abraham Lincoln's first term Vice President from 1861 to 1865. Hamlin had a wonderful working relationship with Lincoln despite the fact that he strongly supported the Radical Republican emancipation agenda. He never allowed these differences to interfere with his and Lincoln's close friendship. Hamlin became Maine's Senator after the Civil War from 1869 to 1881 and was U.S. Minister to Spain from 1881 to 1882.

Albert Sidney Johnston's Favorite Vegetable Beef Chowder

½ pound round steak   2 tbls onion, chopped
2 tbls butter   1 cup potatoes, cubed
2 tsp salt   1 cup carrots, cubed
¼ tsp pepper   2 tbls flour
3 cups water, boiling   4 cups milk
                1 cup cooked peas

Cut round steak into ½ inch cubes and put in cast iron soup kettle with butter. Fry until nicely browned on all sides. Stir frequently to prevent burning. Add 1 teaspoon of salt, pepper, boiling water and onion. Cover kettle and let simmer for 1 hour. Now add potatoes and other teaspoon salt. Cook 20 minutes longer. Blend flour with 2 teaspoons of milk in small wooden mixing bowl. Stir in rest of the milk. Pour this into meat and vegetable mixture in soup kettle. Let simmer, stirring constantly, until soup thickens. Lastly, add peas and stir gently. Serve soup very hot.

** ** ** ** **

Albert Sidney Johnston (1803-62), Confederate General, graduated from West Point in 1826. He fought in the Black Hawk War, resigned from the U.S. Army in 1834, and became commander of the Texas army in 1837. Johnston, a devout Christian from childhood, turned down a Union offer to be General Winfield Scott's second in command. He instead chose to become a full general in the Confederate cause. Jefferson Davis, President of the Confederacy, regarded Johnston to be "the greatest soldier ... then living." Johnston was able to capture Bowling Green, but then suffered losses at Logan Cross Roads, Fort Henry and Fort Donelson. He suffered a serious leg wound at Shiloh on April 6, 1862, the first day of fighting, and subsequently died as a result of this injury. His loss was called "irreparable" by Jefferson Davis.

Mrs. Grant's Corn and Lima Bean Chowder

1 cup lima beans, dried	1 cup celery, diced
6 cups water, cold	1-1/2 cups corn
3 tsp salt	1 tbls sugar
¼ cup butter	Pinch of pepper
2 tbls onion, chopped	3 cups water, boiling
	3 cups milk

Put lima beans in a cast iron soup kettle, cover with water and soak over night. In the morning, drain and cover with 6 cups fresh water. Add 1 teaspoon of the salt and simmer until beans are tender. Meanwhile, melt butter in a cast iron skillet. Add chopped onion and fry until nicely browned. Blend with this the celery, corn, sugar, 2 teaspoons salt, pepper and boiling water. Let simmer ½ hour. Stir this into the soup pot of lima beans along with the milk. Heat thoroughly and serve piping hot. Makes more than enough to feed 6 people.

** ** ** ** **

Ulysses Simpson Grant (1822-85), Union General and 18th President of the United States from 1869 to 1877. He was a brilliant military tactician and relentless warrior, a man who was constantly hammering away at the enemy. Grant was ever persistent, a man of quiet determination and calm resolution. He had all the qualities of a great military leader. Grant, one of many great Christian leaders involved in the Civil War had this to say regarding his beliefs: *"I believe in the Holy Scriptures, and who lives by them will be benefited thereby. Men may differ as to the interpretation, which is human, but the Scriptures are man's best guide ..."*

Killed Lettuce Salad – A Polk Family Favorite

4 slices bacon, diced	6 onions, diced
½ cup vinegar	Salt to suit taste
1 head of lettuce	Pepper to suit taste

Put bacon pieces in a cast iron skillet and fry until nice and crisp but not burned. Drain well in a colander. Add vinegar to the drippings and put back in skillet. Bring to a boil. Meanwhile, chop lettuce into small pieces and put in a large wooden bowl. Then add onions, salt and pepper. Lightly toss. Pour hot vinegar mixture over the mixture and gently stir until everything is nicely blended. Lastly sprinkle crisped bacon pieces on top. Serve immediately.

** ** ** ** **

Confederate Major General Leonidas Polk's (1806-64) father had fought in the War for Independence and had been instrumental in founding the University of North Carolina. Polk was a West Point graduate who was converted while still a cadet. He later resigned his U.S. Army commission to enter the Episcopal ministry. He soon became Bishop of Louisiana. Polk accepted a commission as a Major General at the request of Jefferson Davis (who had been a cadet with him) when the Civil War broke out. He quickly accepted, as he truly believed the South was fighting for a holy cause. He went into combat, with his close friend General Albert Sidney Johnston, at Shiloh in April of 1862. He served the Confederacy while retaining his position in the church. Through an inheritance of his wife's, Polk came to own 400 slaves and established a Sunday school for them. He was killed during the Atlanta Campaign near Marietta, Georgia, when a sharpshooter shot him from his saddle. All through the war his men fondly referred to this kindly man as "Bishop Polk." James Knox Polk, 11th President of the United States, was one of his kinsmen.

Snap Bean Soup – A General Hill Family Favorite

1-1/2 tbls butter	Pinch pepper
2 tbls onion, chopped	1-1/2 cups vegetable juices
2 tbls flour	1 cup snap beans, cooked
1 tsp salt	1-1/2 cups milk

Melt butter in a small cast iron soup kettle and fry the onion for about 5 minutes or until lightly browned. Stir in the flour, salt and pepper. Slowly stir in the vegetable juices. Bring to a boil and let cook for 2 minutes while stirring constantly. Lastly, chop up the snap beans. Add them and the milk. Blend everything well. Serve while steaming hot. Makes enough to serve 5 people.

** ** ** ** **

Daniel Harvey Hill (1821-89) of South Carolina was involved for 7 years in the Mexican War after graduating from West Point. When the Civil War started, he led the Confederate army's 1st North Carolina at Big Bethel. As a major general in March of 1862, Hill commanded a division fighting at Seven Pines, the Seven Days Battles and at South Mountain. This great Christian leader was in charge of defending Richmond during the Gettysburg campaign and was a prominent military leader at both Chickamauga and Chattanooga. Hill's downfall apparently came when he signed a petition recommending that General Braxton Bragg be removed from command due to incompetence. But politics being as they are, instead of Bragg being removed as should have been the case, Hill instead was relieved of his command and transferred to an obscure post in North Carolina. There he eventually surrendered to Union forces with General J.E. Johnston. A great military leader, proven under fire, was virtually destroyed.

Mrs. Lyon's Best Tomato Creamed Soup

4 tbls butter	Pinch of pepper
5 tbls green pepper	2 cups tomato juice, strained
minced	2 tbls flour
1-1/4 tsp salt	2 cups milk, scalded
	Bread crumbs to suit

Melt 2 tablespoons butter in a cast iron skillet. Add minced green pepper. Sauté for 5 minutes. Stir in salt, pepper and tomato juice. Bring to a boil. Now blend together the flour with the other 2 tablespoons butter. Add this to mixture in skillet to thicken. Lastly stir in the milk. Serve with browned and buttered bread crumbs liberally sprinkled over each bowl of hot soup. Makes enough to feed 5 people. Note: Mrs. Lyon sometimes served this soup with popcorn sprinkled over the top. One cup of popcorn was used for each bowl of soup.

** ** ** ** **

Union General Nathan Lyon (1818-1861) was a West Point graduate from Connecticut. He was an outstanding leader of men who had gained a lot of invaluable military experience prior to the beginning of the Civil War. Lyon had already spent much time fighting for his country in the Mexican War, Seminole War and on the frontier. He once made this statement: *"The Bible in which I believe, is no doubt the most wonderful thing God has given Man."* A career soldier, this devout Christian so believed in the preservation of the Union that he willed all his property and belongings to the government in an effort to assist in this effort. Unfortunately, before he could see his dream come to pass, he was killed in action at Wilson's Creek in August of 1861.

3

Tasty Vegetable Dishes from the Long Distant Past

Mrs.John Hunt Morgan's Plantation Style Collard Greens

2 pounds chicken necks	Salt to suit
4 large bunches collard greens, fresh	Pepper to suit
	3 tbls bacon drippings

Put the chicken necks in a large soup kettle and cover with water. Bring to a boil and then let simmer for 20 minutes. Remove chicken necks from pot and set aside. Put the well washed collard greens in the chicken broth. Let simmer until tender. Salt and pepper to taste. Stir in the bacon drippings. Serve while piping hot.

** ** ** ** **

John Hunt Morgan (1825-64) enlisted in the Confederate army when the Civil War broke out and became a scout. So talented was he that he soon thereafter commanded the Kentucky cavalry as a colonel at Shiloh in April of 1862. This young *Bible* believing Christian became known as a raider, taking 400 prisoners in Mississippi and Tennessee. Rewarded by being given command of a brigade, he started out on July 4th on a bold 800-man raid into Union territory. Covering 1000 miles in 24 days, he and his men captured

1200 Union prisoners while losing less than 100 of his own men. Then in December of 1862, during the Stones River campaign, Morgan's raiders captured 1800 prisoners and destroyed more than two million dollars worth of Union military goods. Only two of his men were killed and 24 were wounded. This heroic exploit earned him a promotion to brigadier general and command of a cavalry division. Morgan was finally captured by Federal troops in Lisbon, Ohio, on July 26. He escaped from the Ohio penitentiary in November and again initiated his famous raids. But Morgan's luck ran out and he was killed in Greenville, Tennessee, on September 4, 1864.

Creamed Corn with Green Pepper – A Favorite of the Pelham Family

2 tbls butter	1 tsp sugar
2 tbls flour	1 egg, well beaten
1 cup milk	2 cups fresh corn
1 tsp salt	½ cup green pepper,
Pinch of pepper	chopped fine

Melt the butter in a cast iron skillet or cooking pot. Add flour and blend well. Slowly stir in the milk. Continue stirring until mixture thickens. Then stir in salt, pepper and sugar. Now blend in a small wooden mixing bowl the beaten egg, corn and chopped green pepper. When ready, stir this mixture into the first mixture in the skillet or pot. Cover and bring to a boil. Let simmer together for 20 minutes. Serve while hot.

** ** ** ** **

Lieutenant Colonel John Pelham (1838-63) was, according to General Robert E. Lee, "gallant and courageous" at Fredericksburg. Born in Alabama, this idealistic young soldier resigned his U.S. Army commission and left West Point in 1861 to offer his services to the

Confederate cause. Pelham, a dedicated Christian, was willing to fight and die for the Confederacy. He firmly believed he was fighting in a *"Holy War with the unconditional blessing of God Almighty."* Nevertheless, Pelham was reputed to be quite a handsome ladies man. When this dashing 25-year old officer was killed at Kelley's Ford, at least three lovely Southern belles were known to have gone into mourning.

Baked Eggplant as Prepared and Cooked for Jefferson Davis

2 large egg plants	½ tsp nutmeg
2 tbls onion, minced	1 cup nutmeats, chopped
1 cup celery, chopped	½ cup butter, melted
1 cup bread crumbs	2 cups tomatoes, stewed
½ tsp pepper	2 eggs, well beaten
1 tsp salt	Cream to suit

1 tsp parsley flakes

Put eggplants in large cooking pot and cover with water. Bring to a boil and allow to simmer for 10 minutes. Take eggplants out of the water and slit down their side. Extract and discard the seeds. Lay eggplants in cold, salted water and set aside while preparing the stuffing.

Put minced onion and chopped celery in a buttered cast iron skillet and sauté until nicely browned. Blend these in a wooden mixing bowl with the bread crumbs, pepper, salt, nutmeg, nutmeats, butter, tomatoes and beaten eggs. Lastly, add enough cream to moisten mixture as needed. Fill the cavity of each eggplant with this stuffing. Wind some thread around each eggplant to hold slit shut. Place on the rack of a roasting pan. Put a little water in bottom of pan. Bake at 350 degrees for 25 minutes. Baste with butter and water every few minutes. Stick with a straw to determine when tender. Baste liberally with butter just before removing from the oven. Lastly, lay eggplants on a dish. Now add 3 tablespoons cream to the drippings in bottom of roasting pan. Thicken with a little flour and flavor with parsley flakes. Bring to a quick boil. Pour this mixture over the eggplants and serve immediately.

** ** ** ** **

Jefferson Davis (1808-89), President of the Confederacy, was a man never to be forgotten in American history. He was an individualist, a highly moral man, a man of strong character, a man of unwavering conviction and a dedicated Christian. Davis graduated from the U.S. Military Academy in 1828, one year ahead of Robert E. Lee. He had wished to be made Commander-in-Chief of the Confederate military. Instead, he was inaugurated on February 18, 1861, as provisional President of the Confederate States of America. At the war's end, the orders given to Lieutenant Colonel B.D. Pritchard were: *"Capture or kill Jefferson Davis, the rebel ex-President."* And the editors of *Harper's Weekly* were out for blood: *"Jefferson Davis must be tried for treason. If convicted he must be sentenced. If sentenced he must be executed."*

Braxton Bragg's Special Vegetable Platter

1 head cauliflower	2 bunches snap beans,
4 large carrots,	sliced thin
cut lengthwise	1 tsp salt
2 bunches beets,	2 tbls butter
sliced thin	Cheese to suit,
2 cups brussel sprouts	melted

Put whole cauliflower and sliced up carrots in a large pot with ¼ cup of the water. Cook slowly until tender. Meanwhile, put beets, brussel sprouts and snap beans in another pot with ¼ cup of the water. Also cook slowly until vegetables are tender. Add 1/2 the salt and 1/2 the butter to each pot as the vegetables are cooking. When all vegetables are done, put the whole cauliflower head in the center of a large platter. Arrange the other vegetables around it. Pour hot cheese sauce generously over the cauliflower. Serve while hot.

** ** ** ** **

Braxton Bragg (1817-76), Confederate general, graduated from West Point in 1837 and had a rather distinguished military record early on in his career. He was an advisor to Confederate President Jefferson Davis throughout most of 1864 and joined Davis in his attempt to escape Union forces at the end of the Civil War. But Bragg, a professed Christian, wasn't thought highly of as a military leader later in his career. General E. Kirby Smith and Leonidas Polk both asked Jefferson Davis to relieve Bragg from any command position as early as 1862. General Nathan Bedford Forrest contemptuously cursed Bragg. A soldier's diary, written in 1863, had this to offer: *"General Bragg is not fit for a general ... I believe he is a coward ..."* Dr. D.W. Yandell, an army surgeon, wrote: *"General Bragg is either stark mad or utterly incompetent."*

Mary Surrat's Sweet Potato Baking Secrets

According to Mary Surrat, always select smooth and unblemished sweet potatoes of uniform, medium size, so they will bake in the same length of time. Scrub each sweet potato thoroughly, then dry. Rub each sweet potato lightly with butter. Scoop a small hole from each end and the sweet potatoes will bake more quickly. Bake at 400 degrees for about 1 hour.

Candied Sweet Potato Recipe of Mary Surrat

6 medium size sweet potatoes	¼ cup orange juice
	1 cup dark corn syrup
2 tbls flour	3 tbls butter

Peel the sweet potatoes and put them in a kettle with lightly salted water. Bring to boil and let simmer 15 minutes, or until tender. Drain and lay sweet potatoes in buttered baking pan. Combine flour and orange juice in small mixing bowl. Add corn syrup and blend thoroughly. Pour mixture over sweet potatoes. Dot sweet potatoes with butter. Bake uncovered at 375 degrees for about 1 hour.

** ** ** ** **

Mary Surratt's son, John, was a Confederate spy during the early years of the Civil War. Mary was known to be a decent, Godly woman, who simply ran the boarding house in Washington where John Wilkes Booth and his fellow conspirators met and planned the assassination of President Lincoln. Nevertheless, she was arrested and convicted by a military court of being a Confederate conspirator. She was hanged on July 7, 1865, although there really no evidence that she had any involvement with Booth and the others. Lincoln's Secretary of War, Edwin Stanton, offered a reward of $25,000 for the capture of conspirators John Surratt and David E. Herold. But John escaped his pursuers and fled to Canada after Lincoln's assassination. He finally returned to America in 1867 and was tried but not convicted as his trial resulted in a hung jury.

Lima Beans with Tomatoes – A Wade Family Recipe

1-1/2 cups dry lima beans   6 bacon slices
3 cups cold water   1 medium onion, sliced
1-1/2 cups cooked tomatoes   2 tbls flour
4 whole cloves   ¾ tsp salt
                ¼ tsp pepper

Wash the lima beans and put into a large soup kettle. Cover with water and let soak over night. In the morning, bring to a boil in the water in which they were soaked. Let simmer until tender. Meanwhile, in a separate pot, simmer the tomatoes with the cloves for 10 minutes. Remove cloves and set pot of tomatoes aside. Fry the bacon strips in a cast iron skillet until nice and crisp. Remove bacon and set aside. Brown onion slices in the bacon fat. Stir in the flour, salt and pepper. Blend well. Now add previously cooked tomatoes. Let simmer until thickened. Add lima beans and blend thoroughly. Serve with crisp warm bacon strips laid over the top. Makes enough to feed 6 people.

** ** ** ** **

Benjamin Franklin Wade (1800-78) was a widely known statesman in his day. This man was one of the Radical Republican Senators who joined with virulently anti-Southern Representative Henry W. Davis in drafting a punitive Reconstruction plan in 1864 opposing what they considered to be Lincoln's all to moderate policies toward the South. Wade wanted the South and its leaders severely punished. He later wrote a vindictive manifesto denouncing Lincoln when the President vetoed his extreme measures against his Southern brethren. He was an outspoken, hate-filled, anti-slavery politician who became President Andrew Johnson's acting Vice President in 1865 when Lincoln was assassinated. He vocally opposed this new Presidents more moderate Reconstruction policies as well. Wade was one of the most radical of the abolitionists in his day. Although professing to be a God fearing Christian, he appeared to be quite un-Christian in his attitude and actions toward the South when the War finally ended.

Lincoln's Favorite Childhood Corn Fritters

2 cups fresh corn	1 tsp salt
2 egg yolks, beaten	1 tsp baking powder
1-1/4 cups flour	2 egg whites, beaten stiff

Put the fresh corn in a wooden mixing bowl and stir in the beaten egg yolks. Sift flour, salt and baking powder together and stir into the corn and egg mixture in the mixing bowl. Blend thoroughly. Lastly, fold in the stiffly beaten egg whites. Drop by spoonfuls onto a hot, well greased cast iron skillet. Fry until golden brown. Turn once and fry other side. When done, drain on brown paper bag to absorb excess grease. Serve while piping hot with maple syrup or honey.

** ** ** ** **

According to Isaac N. Arnold, one of Lincoln's close Illinois friends, Abe usually ate very plain food during his childhood. One of the things he was known to eat with some degree of regularity was corn fritters, while wild game put the necessary meat on the dinner table and protein in his diet. The above recipe shows exactly how Lincoln's stepmother, Mrs. Thomas Lincoln, made them for the future President of the United States. Was Abraham Lincoln a Christian? Let his words speak for themselves. This took place when General Lee had marched into Pennsylvania. Everyone in Washington was panic-stricken – everyone, that is, except the President. Lincoln remained perfectly calm. He later explained why to a General who had been wounded at Gettysburg: *"I went to my room. ... and got down on my knees before Almighty God and prayed. ... Soon a sweet comfort crept into my soul that God Almighty had taken the whole business into His own hands."*

** ** ** ** **

4

Stews, Pot Pies and Casseroles from Days Gone By

TheWalker Family Pork and Parsnip Stew

1-1/2 pounds fresh pork   1 quart parsnips, sliced
l large onion, sliced   1- 1/2 tsp salt
1 quart hot water   2 tbls flour
Parsley to suit, chopped

Cut pork into small pieces and put in nice size kettle. Brown the pork in its own fat. Add to this the slices of onion and let cook a few minutes longer. Pour in the hot water and simmer until the pork pieces are nearly tender. Then add the slices of parsnip and salt. Cook for 15 to 20 minutes longer. Meanwhile, blend together the flour and a little cold water. Add this to the meat and vegetables in the kettle. Stir until the stew is thickened. Sprinkle over with chopped parsley and serve piping hot.

** ** ** ** **

Mary Edwards Walker (1832-1919) was the only woman and only civilian to be awarded the **Medal of Honor** during the Civil War. This devout Christian woman was a Union army surgeon who had to work as a nurse on the battlefield because the powers to be wouldn't hire female doctors. Her **Medal of Honor** cites her work at First Manassas. She started at the battle of Chickamauga on September 19-20, 1863. There she served in an army hospital in Chattanooga, Tennessee, where she tirelessly worked as a volunteer surgeon. Dr. Walker often crossed enemy lines to assist victims in need of help. She was once taken prisoner on April 10, 1864, when she accidentally walked into a group of Confederate soldiers. She was released in a trade for a Confederate officer and was thereby able to help as a surgeon during the battle for Atlanta. After the Civil War ended, General W.T. Sherman recommended Dr. Walker for the **Medal of Honor**. She was awarded it in January of 1866. This great lady proudly wore this medal every day until she died.

Millard Fillmore's Favorite Pork Sausage-Apple Casserole

2 pounds pork sausage links
2 cups onions, sliced thin   1/8 tsp cloves, ground
10 apples   ½ cup water
½ cup bread crumbs, dry   ½ cup brown sugar

Put sausage links in a cast iron skillet and fry until nicely browned. Set aside to cool. Spoon off 3 tablespoons of sausage drippings and set aside. Now put sliced onions in the skillet and slowly brown. Cut sausage links into 1-inch pieces. Pare apples and remove cores. Take a deep baking pan and arrange alternate layers of apple slices, sausage chunks and fried onion slices. Sprinkle last layer of apples with cloves and pour the water over this.

Lastly make topping by blending together brown sugar, bread crumbs and 3 tablespoons of the sausage drippings previously set aside. Spread mixture over casserole. Cover dish and bake at 350 degrees for about 45 minutes or until apples are tender. Serve while steaming hot. This recipe will feed 4 to 6 people.

** ** ** ** **

Millard Fillmore (1800-74) was Vice-President under President Zachary Taylor. So dull and wishy washy a politician he was believed to be, that Taylor never even met him until after the election was over. Such a meeting was never arranged, as it wasn't considered to be worth the great General Taylor's time. Yet, Fillmore, proclaiming himself a Christian, still became the 13th President of the United States and served from 1850 to 1853. Today he is best known as the "forgotten" President and remembered historically as being an obscure, colorless individual. He was looked upon as a faceless party hack with few if any opinions of his own.

Chicken Pot Pie as Made by Mrs. McClellan

1 chicken	Pepper to suit taste
Salt to suit taste	3 tbls flour
	1 cup milk

Clean, singe and cut up the chicken. Place it in a cast iron cooking kettle and nearly cover with water. Put lid on the kettle and let simmer gently. An old fowl will require at least 3 or 4 hours slow cooking. A year old chicken should be done in 1-1/2 hours. Remove the cover during the last half-hour of cooking. This will reduce the gravy to about 1-1/2 pints when done. Three-fourths of an hour before time to serve, make dumplings like this:

2 cups flour	1 tsp salt
4 tsp baking powder	2 tbls butter
	1 cup milk

Sift together the flour, baking powder and salt in a wooden mixing bowl. Rub in the butter with the tips of the fingers or chop it in with a knife. Add the milk gradually to make a soft dough. Drop by spoonfuls on top of the boiling liquid in the kettle. Cover tightly and cook slowly for 12 minutes. Do not uncover until dumplings have steamed for a full 12 minutes.

When the dumplings are ready to serve, skim out the chicken pieces and lay them on a platter. Place dumplings on top. Now make the gravy. Add salt and pepper to the broth in the pan. Stir the flour to a paste in the cup of milk. Add this to the liquid in the kettle. Stir until gravy starts to thicken nicely. Pour gravy over the chicken and dumplings on platter. Serve immediately.

** ** ** ** **

General George Brinton McClellan (1826-85), a West Point graduate, class of 1846, was the son of a distinguished Philadelphia surgeon. This man was raised as a boy in a strict Christian atmosphere and later became one of the Union's top military leaders during the Civil War. He saw action at many places including First Bull Run, Rich Mountain and Richmond. General McClellan was the man who soundly defeated the Confederate forces under the command of General Robert E. Lee at Antietam, Maryland, on September 16, 1862. Lee thought highly of Mclellan and considered him to be the best Union commander he had faced during the war. McClellan later got into politics and became Governor of New Jersey, serving in that position from 1878 to 1881.

The McDowell Family Beef Stew Recipe

1-1/2 pounds flank steak	1 pint tomatoes, stewed
or	and strained
rump roast	1 small onion, minced
¼ cup flour	1/3 cup carrots, cubed
1-1/2 tsp salt	1/3 cup turnips, cubed
¼ tsp pepper	4 cups potatoes, quartered

Trim some fat from the meat and heat in a cast iron skillet. Meanwhile, cut meat in cubes of about 1-1/2 inches. Blend flour with salt and pepper in a wooden mixing bowl. Dredge cubes of beef in flour mixture. Put floured cubes in skillet and fry until surface is nicely browned all around. Stir constantly to prevent burning. Turn these browned meat cubes along with the melted fat in which they were browned into a kettle. Add enough boiling water to cover meat. Stir in salt and pepper. Simmer about 3 hours until meat is tender. The tomatoes, onion, carrots and turnips are to be added during the last hour of cooking. Potatoes are to be added 20 minutes before serving. Fifteen minutes before serving, add dumplings to the stew.

Mrs. McDowell's Special Homemade Drop Dumplings

2 cups flour	½ tsp salt
3 tsp baking powder	1 tbls shortening
	¾ cup milk

Sift flour and measure 2 cups. Then sift together in a wooden mixing bowl the flour, baking powder and salt. Cut in the shortening with a knife or the fingers. Add milk to make a good batter. Drop by spoonfuls into boiling liquid in the kettle. Cover closely and cook for about 10 minutes.

The liquid must be kept boiling during the entire 10 minutes. Serve at once. Makes 10 servings.

** ** ** ** **

General Irvin McDowell (1818-85) was born in Ohio into a firmly based Christian family. He went to West Point and graduated at the age of 20 with the class of 1838. McDowell was a favorite of the Lincoln administration, and especially Secretary of the Treasury Salmon P. Chase. Union forces under his command were routed in the battle of First Bull Run near the Manassas railway junction. McDowell was also soundly defeated by Confederate troops led by General Joe Eggleston Johnston and General Beauregard. His came under heavy criticism for his disastrous performance at the battle of Second Bull Run and was relieved of his command. McDowell was exonerated after an investigation but never again given a field command.

Oyster-Sausage Casserole – A Dish Enjoyed by Captain James J. Andrews

1-1/2 cups flour	1 tbls shortening
3 tsp baking powder	½ pint oysters, chopped
½ tsp salt	6 tablespoons oyster juice
	8 pork sausages

Sift together the flour, baking powder and salt in a wooden mixing bowl. Add the shortening and cut in thoroughly with a fork. Add the chopped oysters and the 6 tablespoons oyster juice. Blend everything well. Grease a shallow baking pan. Dump the mixture from the bowl into the baking pan and evenly spread. Prick the sausages and place in two rows on top. Bake at 475 degrees until sausages are nicely browned. Serves 8 people.

** ** ** ** **

James J. Andrews, Union Army Captain bravely led a group of men on a daring raid against the Confederates. This young Bible-toting Christian leader and his brave detachment of soldiers took it upon themselves to steal the *General*, a Confederate locomotive, on April 1, 1862, in an effort to cut the rail lines. But the Confederates in another locomotive, the *Texas*, eventually caught the Union soldiers after a long chase. Nonetheless, the Andrews Raiders had their names forever inscribed in Civil War lore for their incredibly heroic deed. In 1891, the State of Ohio finally erected a special monument in the National Cemetery at Chattanooga, Tennessee, to honor the Andrews Raiders. Eight of these men are buried there. On the marble shaft were placed the names of those oft forgotten heroes.

Navy Bean Casserole – A Favorite of General Philip Kearney

3 cups dried navy beans	1 tsp salt
2 cups corn	¼ tsp pepper
¼ cup cheese, grated	2 tsp bacon drippings
2 cups tomatoes, stewed	½ cup buttered crumbs

Put beans in a soup kettle, cover with water and soak over night. In the morning, cover kettle tightly and bring to a boil. Let simmer until beans are soft. Meanwhile, butter a good-sized baking dish. Arrange alternate layers of navy beans, corn, grated cheese and stewed tomatoes. Add a little of the salt, pepper and bacon drippings to each layer. Cover with crumbs. Bake at 350 degrees for 30 minutes. Makes enough to feed 8 people.

** ** ** ** **

Union General Winfield Scott called Philip Kearney (1814-62) *"The bravest and most perfect soldier"* he had ever known. General Kearney, known to be a devout Bible believing Christian, had an outstanding record during the Civil War. He was a dashing one-armed cavalry officer whose men always rode distinctive dapple-gray horses into battle. He was killed at Chantilly in September of 1862. Met by Confederate troops in the midst of a furious battle, Kearney was asked to surrender. He refused and as he rode away, was shot in the back. The fearless warrior fell from his horse and was dead in an instant. He had died in service to his country – just as he had hoped and prayed to do.

Shepherd Pot Pie as Eaten by the Butterfield Family

4 tbls butter
4 tbls flour
3 tbls onion, chopped
2 cups meat stock
2 tbls green pepper, chopped
1 cup celery, diced
1 cup cooked beef, diced
½ cup cooked carrots, diced
Butter to suit
Mashed potatoes to suit

Melt butter in cast iron kettle. Add onion, green pepper, celery and meat. Slowly cook while stirring constantly until everything is lightly browned. Blend in flour slowly and continue stirring until also browned. Add meat stock and carrots. Blend well. Heat thoroughly. Grease a baking dish. Pour contents of kettle into baking dish and smooth over. Spread on thick covering of mashed potatoes. Dot liberally with butter. Bake at 400 degrees until nicely browned. Makes 6 servings.

** ** ** ** **

Daniel Butterfield, a New York merchant, became a Union Brigadier General in September of 1861. He was awarded the **Medal of Honor** for his heroic actions under fire at Gaine's Mill. This notable Christian military leader was also Chief of Staff to General Joseph Hooker and General George Meade in 1863-1864. And he led a division in General Sherman's historic 1864 March to the Sea. But this man, at age 31, did the one thing he would be most remembered for in history. He composed the notes for the famous bugle call we know even today as **"Taps."** He wrote this at Harrison's Landing, Virginia, to be played at funerals and lights out.

Mrs. Nelson's Corn Casserole

1 tbls butter	1 cup fresh corn
1 onion, grated	4 tomatoes, stewed
1 pound beef, ground	Salt to taste
1 cup corn meal (yellow)	Pepper to taste

Put butter in cast iron skillet and melt. Put onion and meat in skillet and fry on low heat until nicely browned. Then blend in yellow corn meal. Add the corn and stewed tomatoes. Season with salt and pepper to suit taste. Turn into buttered greased casserole dish. Bake at 350 degrees for 1 hour. Serve while hot.

** ** ** ** **

General William Nelson (1824-62) was born in Kentucky and served in the U.S. Navy during the Mexican War. He later joined the Union Army and fought valiantly at Shiloh and Corinth. Always carrying his *Bible* at his side when going into battle, Nelson was wounded during the fighting at Richmond. While getting Louisville ready to thwart off a Confederate attack, Nelson and General Jefferson C. Davis got into a serious argument. Davis became furious and lost control over his commander's rebuke. He pulled out his revolver and mortally wounded Nelson. Davis had friends in high places and thanks to political pressures he went unpunished for his dastardly deed. In fact this murderer was actually allowed to assume a high command position again.

5

Turkeys and Other Old-Time Poultry Dishes

Mrs. Foote's Directions for Properly Roasting Turkey

Dress the turkey. Rinse carefully inside and outside with cold water. Wipe dry. Rub down inside and out with salt and pepper. Set aside and prepare desired stuffing. Fill turkey with stuffing, packing it lightly. Carefully sew up openings and lay turkey on its back in roasting pan. Cover breast of turkey with thin strips of salt pork. Sear in oven at 500 degrees for 15 minutes. Reduce heat to 300 degrees. Take off strips of salt pork. Put cover on roasting pan. Roast until tender. Baste frequently, at least every 15 minutes. Allow about 25 minutes roasting time per pound of turkey.

** ** ** ** **

Rear Admiral Andrew Hull Foote (1806-63), the son of a Connecticut Senator, became a midshipman in 1882. A deeply religious man, he wrote about and spoke out against the slave trade during the 1850s. Foote was a strong believer in the temperance movement. At age 56, he issued orders banning any further rum rations aboard his ship. His was the first U.S. Naval vessel to ever do this. He also influenced the entire United States Navy to follow suit and ban shipboard rations of rum.

The Sherman Family's Chicken Fricassee Recipe

2 - 3 pound chickens	½ tsp pepper
2 large onions, sliced	8 tbls flour
2 tsp salt	¾ cup cold water

Put both whole chickens in large kettle with sliced onions. Cover with boiling water. Let simmer until half done. Add salt and pepper. Continue cooking until tender. Take chickens out of broth. Remove skin and take out bones. Leave chicken meat in fairly large pieces and set aside. Now blend flour with cold water and make smooth paste. Add this to broth in kettle and thicken for gravy. Bring to a boil. Add the chicken meat and stir well. Serve with squash biscuits (see Chapter 13). Feeds 8 people.

** ** ** ** **

General William Tecumseh Sherman (1820-91), son of an Ohio Supreme Court Justice, led his Union troops to victory in Charleston, South Carolina, on February 18, 1865. He soundly thrashed Confederate General Beauregard and occupied the beautiful city. Sherman was without a doubt one of the greatest of all Union generals in the Civil War. As he started his famous March to the Sea on November 15,

1864, he told General Grant: *"I can make Georgia howl."* He then proceeded to march his 60,000-man army through the interior of Georgia, cutting a 60-mile wide swath of indescribable devastation and destruction. Orphaned at the age of 9, this man was raised by a wealthy friend of his father. He went on to graduate near the top of his class at West Point in 1840. Brought up in a Christian centered family, Sherman was taught to never doubt the infallibility of the Bible, or as he was to say, *"Jesus Christ, my Saviour."*

The Mosby Family's Skillet Southern Fried Chicken

3 pound frying chicken	4 cups flour
1 cup lard	6 tsp salt
	2 tsp pepper

Cut up the frying chicken. Melt the lard in a large cast iron skillet. Put the flour, salt and pepper in a brown paper bag. Close and shake heartily to blend everything well. Place a number of chicken pieces in bag and shake. Take out the pieces of chicken and put in medium hot fat in skillet. Fry on one side 10 minutes. Lower the heat. Cover skillet. Cook 5 minutes longer. Uncover. Cook a little longer to make crispier. Take chicken pieces out of skillet. Set on another flattened brown paper bag and allow to drain.

Mrs. Mosby's Special Gravy To Go With Her Fried Chicken

After finishing frying chicken, drain the fat (grease) from the skillet. Set aside for making gravy as follows:

3 tbls fat	1 cup water
3 tbls flour	Salt to suit taste
1 cup milk	Pepper to suit taste

First carefully scrape the bottom and sides of the cast iron skillet for the crusts left behind from frying the chicken pieces. Then add the fat and stir in flour. Cook on low heat for a couple minutes while stirring constantly. Now stir in milk and water. Add a little flour if necessary to thicken more. Salt and pepper to suit taste. Cook 3 to 4 minutes longer. Serve over mashed potatoes or hot biscuits. Some people enjoy this gravy spooned over their fried chicken pieces as well.

** ** ** ** **

Captain John Singleton Mosby (1833-1916) was a widely known, heroic and dashing young Christian cavalry officer who fearlessly fought for the Confederacy. On March 9, 1863, he pulled off a daring exploit in Virginia, only 20 miles from Washington. He and 29 of his men raided the Union camp at Fairfax Court House and captured General Edwin Stoughton, 2 captains, 30 soldiers and 58 horses. Not one Confederate cavalryman was wounded or killed in this escapade. So elusive was Mosby during the Civil War that he became known as *"The Gray Ghost."* Mosby's deeds earned him an awesome reputation as a fearless man of action. And so dangerous were he and his raiders to the Union cause that General Grant once gave orders that he be hanged if captured. They later became friends and Mosby was one of his major political supporters.

George Washington Custis Lee's Family Recipes For Roasting Fowl

Chicken: Having dressed a chicken, stuff it, using the Lee family *Old Fashioned Stuffing* given below. *"Truss the bird by crossing the drumsticks, tying them with a long string and then tying to the tail. Fasten the wings close to the body with a skewer, draw the skin at the neck under the back and pin with another skewer. Then turn the bird on its breast and draw string, which is fastened to tail around skewers, fasten it and cut it. Rub chicken with salt and rub breast and legs with butter and flour worked together. Place in roasting pan and sprinkle bottom of pan with flour. Place pan in oven at 350 degrees until flour is browned. Then lower to 300 and baste often. Melt butter half the size of an egg in ¾ cup hot water and use for basting while it lasts. Then use fat from roasting pan. Turn bird occasionally so it may brown evenly on all sides. Cook until breast meat is tender, which will be about 1-1/2 hours for a 4 pound chicken. Remove strings and skewers and serve."*

Turkey: Proceed as with roast chicken using twice as much *Old Fashioned Stuffing*. A turkey weighing 10 pounds will be done roasting in approximately 3 hours.

Goose: Dress a goose, washing and scrubbing it with a brush and hot soapsuds. Rinse thoroughly in cold water and then dry. Stuff with *Old Fashioned Stuffing* given below. Sprinkle all over with salt and pepper and lay 5 or 6 thin strips of fatty salt pork on the breast. Bake at 350 degrees for 2 hours, basting often with fat from bottom of roasting pan. Remove the salt port strips before goose is done. Serve with applesauce.

Wild Duck: Clean and prepare as a goose, using less salt pork. Stuff with *Old Fashioned Stuffing*. Bake about ½ hour, starting at 375 degrees, then reducing to 350 degrees. Serve with currant jelly

The Lee Family Old Fashioned Stuffing

Simply blend the following ingredients together in a large wooden mixing bowl:

2 cups hot mashed potatoes	1/3 cup butter
1-1/4 cups soft bread crumbs	1 egg
¼ cup fat salt pork, chopped	1-1/2 tsp salt
1 onion, chopped fine	1 tsp sage

** ** ** ** **

George Washington Custis Lee (1832-1913), the eldest son of General Robert E. Lee, was raised in a strongly rooted Christian family. A brilliant scholar, he graduated first in his 1854 class at West Point and in 1861 received a commission in the army of the Confederacy. Lee quickly rose to the rank of General and spent most of the Civil War in the trusted position as aide-de-camp to Confederate President Jefferson Davis. And as we all know, Jefferson Davis was also known to be a man of unwavering Christian convictions. After the Civil War ended, Lee taught engineering for a time at the prestigious Virginia Military Institute. He eventually followed in his father's footsteps and became President of Washington College (presently Washington and Lee College) in 1871.

The Wirz Family Instructions for Properly Roasting Duck

Dress duck and rinse carefully inside and out with cold water. Wipe dry. Rub all around, both inside and out, with salt and pepper. Set aside and make special stuffing of peeled and quartered apples mixed with ½ cup raisins. Fill ducks cavity with this stuffing. Carefully sew up opening. Lay duck on its back on rack of roasting pan. Baste liberally with orange juice. Sear in oven at 500 degrees for 15 minutes. Then reduce the heat to 300 degrees. Cover roasting pan. Roast duck until tender. Continue to baste with orange juice every 10 minutes. Allow 20 to 25 minutes roasting time per pound of duck. Serve with cranberry sauce and sweet potatoes.

Here's a second Wirz family recipe for preparing wild duck:

2 mallard ducks	1 cup raisins
Bacon strips to suit	Salt as needed
6 red tart apples,	Pepper as needed
quartered	Spices of choice

Dress both ducks and rinse with cold water inside and out. Wipe dry. Liberally sprinkle with salt and pepper both inside and out. Stuff ducks with a mixture of the apples and raisins. Sew up opening. Place ducks on rack of roasting pan, breast facing up. Pack rest of apples and raisins around them. Sprinkle ducks with whatever spices you like. Place bacon strips on each duck. Pour 2 cups water into bottom of roasting pan. Bake at 350 degrees until ducks are tender. Add more water to pan if required. When ducks are done, flour can be added to pan drippings to make delicious gravy.

** ** ** ** **

Captain Henry Wirz (1822-65), a Christian physician, was born in Switzerland and immigrated to the United Stated in 1849. He was wounded during the Civil War at Seven Pines. Later on, after returning from a Confederate mission to Europe in 1864, Wirz was assigned the unsavory job as commandant of Andersonville, the notorious Confederate prison camp in Georgia. Thirteen thousand Federal prisoners died at Andersonville due to overcrowding, terrible sanitation and lack of shelter. This man was unfairly tried and convicted of *"murder, in violation of the laws and customs of war."* Captain Wirz was hanged on November 10, 1865, in the old Capitol Prison at the foot of Capitol Hill in Washington. He was the only person executed for "war crimes" after the Civil War ended.

Captain Buchanan's Favorite Spanish Chicken Dish

3 pound chicken	1 tbls chili powder
2 tbls flour	½ tsp salt
4 fresh tomatoes, skinned	1 medium onion, diced
	Cayenne pepper to suit
1 cup cooked rice	½ cup bread crumbs

Cut up chicken into pieces suitable for frying. Put pieces into well greased cast iron skillet. Fry until nicely browned all around. Take chicken pieces out of skillet and set aside in a baking dish. Then make gravy by adding a little water and flour in the skillet. Stir constantly until gravy thickens. Pour this over the chicken pieces in baking dish. Now stir together the tomatoes, rice, chili powder, salt and onion in a wooden mixing bowl. Pour this mixture over the chicken and gravy in the baking dish. Sprinkle with cayenne pepper to taste. Bake for 1 hour at 350 degrees. Cover with bread crumbs and bake 30 to 40 minutes longer. Serve while steaming hot.

** ** ** ** **

Franklin Buchanan (1800-74) was born in Maryland and served in the U.S. Navy. He assisted in the planning of the United States Naval Academy in 1845 under Secretary of the Navy George Bancroft. He saw action during the Mexican War and was with Commodore Perry on his China/Japan expedition from 1852 to 1855. A born again Christian and a Southern sympathizer, Buchanan resigned from the U.S. Navy in 1861 and joined the Confederate Navy as a Captain. He was given command of the *CSS Virginia* (the rebuilt *USS Merrimac*). Buchanan was wounded during the battle in which he captured the *USS Congress*. He was in command of the Confederate squadron defeated by Admiral Farragut in the famous August 1864 Battle of Mobile Bay.

The Ambrose Powell Hill Family Roast Turkey

Clean and singe the feathers of the freshly killed turkey. Wash thoroughly both inside and out. Lightly pack turkey with desired stuffing and sew up openings. Place on a rack in roasting pan, breast facing up. Brush with melted butter. Sprinkle with flour. Bake at 400 degrees until flour starts to brown. Then reduce oven heat to 325 degrees. Pour 5 tablespoons melted butter and 2/3 cup boiling water into roasting pan and mix with drippings from turkey. Season with salt and pepper to suit taste. Use this to baste turkey every 10 to 15 minutes. Let roast about 1 hour for every 3 pounds of turkey. A 12-pound turkey requires about 4 hours roasting time. Serve with brown gravy and cranberry sauce.

** ** ** ** **

General Ambrose Powell Hill (1825-65), born in Culpeper, Virginia, struggled mightily to get through West Point, but he finally graduated in 1848. This fine Christian leader turned out to be a top-notch soldier who saw much action during the Civil War. He fought bravely in many important battles including the Peninsular Campaign, Williamsburg, Mechanicsville, Gaine's Mill, Cedar Mountain, Antietam and Sharpsburg to name but a few. He was wounded at Chancellorsville. Later, as General Grant was launching his final assault on Petersburg, General Hill was shot and killed as he fearlessly rode to the front lines to rally his men. This was in all probability best, for Hill had previously remarked that he did not want to be alive to witness the end of the Confederacy.

6

A Variety of Stuffings from Another Era

John Worden's Favorite Sausage-Chestnut Stuffing

1 pound pork sausage
1 large onion, minced
1-1/2 cups coarse breadcrumbs
1 cup cooked chestnuts, crushed
1 stalk celery, chopped fine
1 tbls parsley, chopped fine
2 tsp sage
1/4 tsp pepper
½ tsp salt
1 egg, well beaten
2 tbls sherry wine

Crumble the sausage in a cast iron skillet with the minced onion and fry until the onion is nicely browned. Take a wooden mixing bowl and combine the bread crumbs, chestnuts, celery, parsley, sage, pepper and salt. Blend everything well. Then mix the fried sausage and onion with this. Add the beaten egg and sherry wine. Mix thoroughly. If stuffing isn't moist enough, add more of the sherry as required.

** ** ** ** **

John Lorimer Worden (1818-1897), was an obscure Union naval officer from New York with 25 years of military service when the Civil War broke out. He was a Christian whose life did a complete and unexpected turn around when he was given command of the *U.S.S. Monitor*. As a result, Worden gained unexpected national celebrity after he defeated the *C.S.S. Merrimac* in the historic naval battle on March 9, 1862. In early 1863, this man was given command of the *USS Montauk* and became part of the South Atlantic Blockading Squadron. He was later appointed Superintendent of Naval Academy (Annapolis) from 1869 to 1874 and then finally retired in 1886 as a Rear Admiral.

The Ewell Family's Best Giblet Stuffing

1 cup turkey giblets, chopped

2 tsp poultry seasoning	½ tsp parsley, chopped
2 cups soft bread cubes	2 tbls turkey pan drippings
3 tbls celery, diced	Salt to suit taste
1 tsp onion, chopped	Pepper to suit taste
Sage to suit taste	Turkey broth as needed

Combine all of the ingredients in a wooden mixing bowl and stir thoroughly. Add turkey broth enough to get the desired consistency for the stuffing. Squeeze together between the fingers until all is nicely blended.

** ** ** ** **

Confederate General Richard Stoddert Ewell (1817-72) was trained at West Point and began his military career as an Indian fighter. He gained even more valuable experience by also fighting valiantly in the Mexican War. Ewell decided to join with the Confederacy and became a Brigadier General in June of 1861. He was severely wounded and lost a leg in the battle at Groveton in August of 1862. Despite this terrible handicap, this outstanding Christian military leader was so highly regarded that he was still given a command position preceding the Second Battle of Manassas. Best known as the "fighting General," he was once again struck by a bullet during the Battle of Gettysburg. This time he laughingly declared to his troops that this one didn't hurt. He'd taken the bullet in his wooden leg! Ewell saw lots of action during the Civil War at such places as Winchester, First Bull Run, Cedar Mountain, Cross Keys, Wilderness, Gettysburg and others. General Sherman captured him at Sayler's Creek in April of 1865. After the war was finally over, Ewell became a farmer in Nashville.

Abner Doubleday's Giblet Corn Meal Stuffing

1 cup giblets, cut up   1 large onion, minced
3 cups turkey broth   1 egg, beaten
¾ cup corn meal   1 tbls poultry seasoning
3 cups bread cubes   Sage to suit taste
¾ cup celery, chopped   Salt to suit taste
Pepper to suit taste

Put cut up giblets and turkey broth in soup kettle and bring to a boil. Slowly stir in corn meal. Let cook for 10 minutes while stirring constantly. Then add bread cubes, celery, onion, beaten egg and poultry seasoning. Blend everything well. Lastly add sage, salt and pepper to suit taste. More broth may be added if necessary to get desired consistency of the stuffing.

** ** ** ** **

Major General Abner Doubleday (1819-1893), a New York native, graduated from West Point. He was involved militarily in the Mexican and Seminole Wars. Doubleday was the man who, while on garrison duty, fired the first shot from Fort Sumter. He fought gallantly in the Shenandoah Campaign and won regular promotions. This fine soldier also fought bravely at such places as Second Bull Run, Antietam and Fredericksburg. Doubleday, who was raised in a stalwart Christian family, was given temporary command of I Corps when General John Reynolds was killed during the Battle of Gettysburg in 1863. This is the same man who was to later become famous as the founder of our national pastime – baseball. He is widely credited with inventing the game in 1839 although some sport's authorities and historians dispute this.

General Pemberton's Favorite Mushroom Stuffing

1 cup mushrooms, chopped	1 tsp poultry seasoning
2 cups soft bread crumbs	2 tbls butter
3 tbls celery, diced	Turkey broth, as needed
1 tsp onion, chopped	Salt to suit taste
½ tsp parsley, chopped	Pepper to suit taste

Take a large wooden mixing bowl and stir in the mushrooms, bread crumbs, celery, onion, parsley and poultry seasoning. Work in the butter with a fork. Slowly add enough turkey broth to get the desired consistency for the stuffing. Season with salt and pepper to suit taste.

** ** ** ** **

Lieutenant General John Clifford Pemberton (1814-81), a lifelong Christian, was born into an old established Philadelphia Quaker family. He graduated from West Point, refused a U.S. commission as a colonel, and instead joined the Confederate army in April of 1861. Pemberton was the man who heroically defended Vicksburg, Mississippi, against General Ulysses Grant's siege that began on May 18,

1863. He was ultimately defeated and forced to accept Grant's "unconditional surrender" terms on July 4. In this humiliating defeat, many Southerners, because of his northern family ties, suspected Pemberton of some sort of underhanded treachery. Nevertheless, Fort Pemberton, constructed in Greenwood, Mississippi, was eventually named in his honor.

Sally Louisa Tompkins' Oyster Stuffing

1 pint oysters	½ tsp salt
3 cups bread crumbs	¼ tsp pepper
¼ cup butter, melted	1 tbls lemon juice

Drain the juice off the oysters and set aside, as it may be needed later. Cut oysters into quarters and put pieces into a wooden mixing bowl. Add breadcrumbs, melted butter, salt, pepper and lemon juice. Blend these ingredients thoroughly. If more moisture is required, simply add some of the oyster juice previously set aside.

** ** ** ** **

Sally Louisa Tompkins (1833-1916) grew up in a wealthy ChristianVirginia family. She devoted her life as a young woman to taking care of the sick. When the Civil War broke out, this young woman took it upon herself to open a hospital in Richmond. President of the Confederacy, Jefferson Davis, commissioned her a Captain in the military when the government officially took over all medical services. Sally is the *only* woman to ever have been awarded a regular commission in the Confederate Army. Her untiring work in helping others in time of great need never ceased as it even continued after the tragic Civil War ended.

Julia Ward Howe's Corn Meal Stuffing

3 cups turkey broth	1 tbls poultry seasoning
½ cup corn meal	1 egg, well beaten
3 cups soft bread cubes	Sage to suit taste
¾ cup celery, diced	Salt to suit taste
1 large onion, chopped	Pepper to suit taste

Put turkey broth in a cast iron kettle and bring to a boil. Gradually stir in the corn meal. Let it cook for a full 10 minutes while stirring constantly. Then add bread cubes, diced celery, chopped onion, poultry seasoning and well beaten egg. Blend everything thoroughly. Season to taste with sage, salt and pepper. Add a little more turkey broth or hot water if needed to get the desired consistency of the stuffing.

** ** ** ** **

Julia Ward Howe (1819-1910) of Boston was a poet, writer and reformer. This God-fearing woman was inspired to write the lyrics to the immortal *"Battle Hymn of the Republic"* while touring Union Army camps around Washington, D.C. Her poem first appeared in the February 1862 issue of *The Atlantic Monthly*. The editor gave the poem its name. Mrs. Howe apparently wrote her poem to fit a familiar melody from the nineteenth century by William Steffe. It was at the time popularly sung by Union soldiers as a rousing song known as "John Brown's body lies a moldering in the grave." Mrs. Howe was the first female to ever have been elected to membership in the prestigious *American Academy of Arts and Letters*. She was also widely acclaimed to be an excellent cook when time permitted. The above recipe was one of her favorites.

Mrs. Richardson's Special Oyster Stuffing

1-1/2 cups oysters, quartered	1 tsp poultry seasoning
1 cup celery, diced	2 tbls turkey drippings
1 tsp onion, chopped	Salt to suit taste
2-1/2 cups soft bread cubes	Pepper to suit taste
½ tsp parsley, chopped	Turkey broth as required

Put all of the above ingredients, except for the turkey broth, in a large wooden mixing bowl. Using the fingers, work them together until everything in completely blended. Lastly, add the turkey broth, a little at a time, as needed while kneading the mixture. Continue this until the desired consistency is reached for a good stuffing.

** ** ** ** **

Albert Deane Richardson (1833-69) was a newspaperman who came south incognito to cover the secession crisis. He decided to stay on to cover the beginning of the Civil War fighting in Virginia and the West. Confederate soldiers near Vicksburg, Mississippi captured Richardson, a professed Christian, in May of 1863. He subsequently escaped after spending 18 long months in prison. This brave man then proceeded to walk 400 miles to freedom. Richardson's freedom was short lived however. He was later shot and killed by a jealous husband in the *New York Tribune* newsroom.

7

Delicious Old Time Meat Cookery

John Ericsson's Favorite Kjoet Boller (Swedish Meat Balls)

1 pound ground beef	½ tsp pepper
1 pound ground pork	2 tsp salt
1 pint milk	½ tsp ground cloves
2 eggs	¼ tsp allspice
1 large onion, chopped fine	

Use good meat such as ground chuck or round steak. Put all the ingredients in a large wooden mixing bowl and mix thoroughly. The more milk worked in, the softer the meatballs will be. Form into small balls (about 40 from this recipe) while dipping the fingers into cold water to make handling easier. Do not roll the meatballs in flour! Melt some butter or other fat (it's best to use equal parts of butter and bacon fat) in a large cast iron skillet. Put in the meatballs and fry until nicely browned all over. When browned, take from skillet and put in casserole dish or baking pan. Set aside while making gravy by adding hot water, salt and pepper to suit taste to the fat left in the skillet. Slowly stir in enough flour to thicken. When done, pour gravy over meatballs. Cover and let simmer on stove or bake at 300 degrees for 1 hour. This recipe serves 8 people.

** ** ** ** **

John Ericsson (1803-89) was a brilliant engineer and inventor who immigrated to the United States from Sweden in 1839. He designed the *Princeton* in 1844, the first warship ever built to have underwater propellers. This devout Christian was also the man who designed the Union's ironclad *USS Monitor* which took only 100 days to build and was launched in January of 1862. This ship was outfitted with a revolving gun turret, a first in naval warfare. After the Confederate ironclad frigate *CSS Merrimac* had sunk the *USS Cumberland*, it had to withdraw from battle when going up against the *USS Monitor* on March 9, 1862.

Beef Loaf Specialty of the Wilson Family

1-1/2 pound ground round steak	2 tsp celery, chopped
2 eggs	Dash of thyme
1-1/2 cups bread crumbs	Dash of sage
2 tbls onion, chopped fine	2 tbls salt
2 tbls parsley, chopped	½ tsp pepper

Put ground round steak in large wooden mixing bowl with the eggs, bread crumbs, onion, celery and the spices. Thoroughly blend together by working with fingers. Place in bread pan and pack firmly until mixture is firmly molded to shape of pan. Run knife blade around loaf. Turn it out onto roasting pan or flat baking tin. Place in oven and bake at 350 degrees for 2 hours. Baste every 15 minutes with hot stock. When done, set side to cool. Cut into thin slices and serve cold with horseradish and hard-boiled eggs.

** ** ** ** **

Major General James Harrison Wilson (1837-1925), an 1860 West Point graduate, was known to be an outstanding Christian leader in the Union Army. He was a brilliant commander, a daring officer and was the instigator of many spectacular military raids during the Siege of Petersburg. General Wilson served under the great General W.T. Sherman and General George McClellan, and he led a cavalry corps from 1864 to 1865. He capped his heroic career off with a phenomenally successful Selma raid and a sensational finale – the capture of Confederate President Jefferson Davis.

Mrs. Early's Corned Beef Boiled Dinner

4 pounds corned beef   3 parsnips, quartered
4 quarts cold water   4 large carrots, quartered
3 large onions, quartered 3 large potatoes, quartered
2 large turnips, quartered 1 small cabbage, quartered

Put corned beef into large kettle with cold water and bring to boil. Drain off water. Add 4 more quarts cold water. Again bring to boil. Let simmer until meat is tender. Take meat from kettle and taste liquid. If too salty, pour some off and add enough fresh water to make at least 2 quarts of good tasting broth. To this broth add onions. Cook 30 minutes. Then add turnips, parsnips, carrots, potatoes and cabbage. Cook 20 to 30 minutes more, or until all vegetables are tender. Lastly, put corned beef back in kettle with vegetables and reheat. Serve this boiled dinner on large platter. Put corned beef in center with drained vegetables placed neatly around it.

** ** ** ** **

General Jubal Anderson Early (1816-94) of Franklin County, Virginia, graduated from West Point and initially saw action in the Seminole War. This warrior, who always read passages from his Bible before going into battle, joined the Confederate Army and led the 24th Virginia at First Bull Run. He participated in skirmishes during the Peninsular Campaign and was wounded at Williamsburg. Early fought at Antietam, Fredericksburg, Chancellorsville and Gettysburg to name but a few of his other battlefield endeavors. He also led a cavalry force in an attempt to capture Washington for the Confederacy on July 9, 1864, but Union forces under the command of General "Lew" (Lewis) Wallace blocked his heroic efforts. Wallace was actually defeated on the battlefront, but he was able to successfully hold off Early's assault until General Ulysses S. Grant could get there and save the day.

The Grierson Family's Upside Down Beef Pie

1-1/2 cups flour	¼ tsp white pepper
3 tsp baking powder	5 tbls shortening
1 tsp salt	¾ cup milk
1 tsp paprika	¼ cup onion, sliced
1 tsp celery salt	1 cup tomatoes, crushed

¾ pound ground beef

Sift together in a wooden mixing bowl the flour, baking powder, ½ teaspoon salt, paprika, celery salt and white pepper. Chop in with a fork 3 tablespoons of the shortening until it is mixed thoroughly. Add milk and stir until well blended.

Melt remaining 2 tablespoons shortening in 9-inch cast iron skillet. Put in onions and fry until soft. Add crushed tomatoes, remaining salt and ground beef. Bring to boil. Take skillet off stove. Spread mixture from mixing bowl on top of meat mixture in skillet. Put skillet in oven and bake at 475 degrees for about 20 minutes. Turn out of skillet upside down on large plate or platter. Serves 8 people.

** ** ** ** **

Early in April of 1863, a cavalry group comprised of 1700 men known as Grierson's brigade swept down from Mississippi to join with other Union units in southern Louisiana. They rode under the command of Benjamin Henry Grierson (1826-1911), a hard riding, Bible believing Christian, who had been commissioned a major in the cavalry in October 1861. They were virtually unopposed, as most Confederate soldiers had been sent to fight in Tennessee. In this 600 mile trek, Grierson and his men confiscated around 1,000 horses and mules, took 500 Confederate prisoners, and inflicted close to 100 casualties. And they were able to destroy approximately 50 miles of railroad lines. All of this was accomplished at the cost of only 24 casualties from Grierson's unit. Grierson was eventually promoted to the rank of Major General.

Beef Pot Roast as Made for Jefferson Davis

¼ cup flour   1 pint boiling water
1 tsp salt   2 cloves
½ tsp pepper   3 medium onions, quartered
3 pound chuck roast   5 potatoes, quartered
1-1/2 tbls fat   5 carrots, cut in pieces

Blend flour with the salt and pepper in large wooden mixing bowl. Dredge chuck roast in flour mixture and set aside momentarily. Melt the fat (lard or butter) in a large cast iron kettle. Then put roast in kettle and brown on all sides. Add boiling water and cloves. Cover and let simmer for about 2 hours. Then add onions, potatoes and carrots to gravy in kettle with roast. Cover and let simmer together for another 30 to 60 minutes or until meat is tender and vegetables are done.

** ** ** ** **

Jefferson Davis (1808-1889), President of the Confederacy, was a devout Christian man who unquestionably believed that the *Bible* was the infallible word of God. He was a hero in the South during and after the Civil War and remains so even today. After his capture, the editors of *Harper's Weekly* were vengeful: ***"Mr. Davis*** *must be tried for treason.   If convicted he must be sentenced.   If sentenced he must be hanged."* They and many others in the North were full of hatred for a truly great and Godly Southern gentleman.   Davis was captured by a Union cavalry detachment and wrongly imprisoned for two years at Fortress Monroe.   Although harshly treated and often mistreated, he survived his ordeal.   The only things Davis was allowed to read while in prison were his *Bible* and his *Episcopal Prayer book.* This great Christian was never brought to trial and was finally released after many public outcries.   Many notable individuals helped financially to secure his release from prison.   They included such people as Cornelius Vanderbilt, a man who made $10 million in the steamboat industry during the Civil War, and Horace Greeley, the famed journalist with the *New York Tribune.*

General Schofield's Secret Family Meat Loaf Recipe

1 egg, well beaten   1 tsp salt
½ cup tomatoes, crushed ½ tsp pepper
½ cup celery, chopped   ½ pound ground chuck
½ cup onion, minced   ½ pound ground pork
1 cup soft bread crumbs ½ pound ground pork liver
4 slices bacon

Put eggs, tomatoes, celery, onion and bread crumbs in large wooden mixing bowl. Stir until bread crumbs are soaked and everything is nicely blended. Add salt and pepper. Lastly work in the ground chuck, pork and pork liver with fingers until everything is thoroughly mixed. Pack into well greased loaf pan. Cut bacon slices in half. Lay pieces over meat loaf. Bake at 375 degrees for 1-1/2 hours. Serves 6 to 8 people

** ** ** ** **

General John McAllister Schofield (1831-1906), son of a Baptist minister, attended West Point and graduated in 1853. He was but 33 years old during the Battle of Franklin on November 30, 1864, just south of Nashville. This terrible encounter ended in disaster for Confederate General John Bell Hood who decided to make a frontal assault: Confederate dead: 1,750 – wounded: 3,800. Union dead: 189 – wounded: 1,033. Schofield also fought at Wilson's Creek and was with General Sherman on his March through the Carolinas in 1865. This man, a Christian since childhood, later served as Secretary of War in 1868-69. He was also the superintendent at West Point from 1876-81.

How Mrs. Chase Prepared Yorkshire Steak

1-1/2 pound round steak – 1 inch thick

Season steak with salt and pepper. Place is greased baking dish or roasting pan. Brown in oven at 550 degrees for 5 minutes. Make **Yorkshire Pudding** and pour over browned steak. Reduce heat to 475 degrees and bake 15 minutes longer. Serves 6 people nicely.

Mrs. Chase's Yorkshire Pudding Recipe

1-1/2 cups flour	2 egg yolks, beaten well
2 tsp baking powder	1 cup milk
½ tsp salt	2 egg whites, beaten stiffly

1/3 cup hot beef drippings

Sift together the flour, baking powder and salt in a wooden mixing bowl. Blend in egg yolks. Add milk. Mix everything thoroughly. Fold in stiff egg whites. Pour mixture over browned Yorkshire steak as directed above, or pour into shallow baking pan containing hot beef drippings. Bake at 475 degrees for about 20 minutes. Cut into squares and serve with hot Yorkshire Steak.

** ** ** ** **

Salmon Portland Chase (1808-73) was a Dartmouth College graduate who practiced law in Cincinnati. He gained quite a reputation for himself by defending escaped slaves. Chase, a Christian, became President Lincoln's Secretary of the Treasury from 1861 to 1864. It was in 1864 that he ordered *"In God We Trust"* was to be printed on every piece of U.S. currency. Chase was Chief Justice of the U.S. Supreme Court from 1864 to 1873. He was often at odds with Lincoln as he considered the President to be an administrative incompetent. And he felt Lincoln was unduly moderate in handling the prosecution of the Civil War against the South.

8

Delightful Desserts from the Civil War Period

General Butler's Favorite Bread Pudding

¼ cup sugar   ¼ tsp cinnamon
¼ tsp salt   1 egg, slightly beaten
½ tsp vanilla   2 cups milk, scalded
2 tbls butter, melted   1 cup bread cubes
½ cup raisins

Combine together in a wooden mixing bowl the sugar, salt, vanilla, melted butter, cinnamon and beaten egg. Blend these ingredients well. Slowly add the scalded milk while stirring constantly. Lastly add bread cubes and raisins. Mix together thoroughly. Pour into well buttered baking pan. Set baking pan in a larger pan of warm water. Bake at 350 degrees for about 1 hour or until inserted knife blade comes out clean. Let cool before serving. Serve with heavy cream. Makes enough to feed 4 people.

** ** ** ** **

Major General Benjamin Franklin Butler (1818-93) became Governor of New Orleans in May of 1862. He was evidently a dictatorial, extremely corrupt, and power mad individual. He ordered a man hanged for merely taking down a Union flag. And he gave what was known at the time as his notorious *"Woman Order."* This so called Butler's law declared that any female caught insulting a Union military man would be punished as a prostitute. His many notorious actions created international protests and Butler was removed from office in December of 1862. Butler, a man who professed himself a Christian, had friends in high places and subsequently became a General in the Union Army. He led a military force in 1865 under orders to capture Fort Fisher on the coast of North Carolina. The mission failed due to Butler's incompetence as a military leader. As a consequence, he was relieved of his command. Butler was considered to be the typical worthless politically appointed general who was of dubious value to the Union cause.

The Forrest Family Molasses Pie Recipe

3 egg yolks	½ tsp salt
1-1/2 cups molasses	1 tbls flour
2 tbls butter, melted	1 tbls cornstarch
¾ cup brown sugar	3 egg whites
½ tsp nutmeg	1 cup pecans
½ cup cinnamon	Sugar to suit

Put egg yolks in wooden mixing bowl and beat until thick. Stir in molasses and melted butter. Combine sugar, nutmeg, cinnamon, salt, flour and cornstarch in separate bowl. Stir together and blend with first mixture. Set aside while egg whites are beaten until fluffy. Fold egg whites into previous mixture. Pour into pastry lined pie pan. Bake at 425 degrees for about 15 minutes. Take pie from oven and cover with generous layer of pecans. Sprinkle with sugar. Put back in oven and bake 15 minutes longer.

** ** ** ** **

The name of General Nathan Bedford Forrest (1821-77) became so famous during the Civil War that it symbolized the entire Confederate cause. The Union decided that this heroic Southern leader must at all costs be stopped. Forrest, brought up in a fundamental Christian home, was without doubt one of the most outstanding cavalry leaders in the entire war. He was seriously wounded in April of 1862. But Forrest recovered and went on to a phenomenal military career that would bring him fame as probably the greatest, most aggressive, and best known cavalry raider of the Civil War. So feared was Forrest that General Sherman swore to stop him *"if it costs ten thousand lives and bankrupts the federal treasury."* But even Sherman had little success in this regard.

Raspberry Cream Pie – A Schurz Family Specialty

Raspberries to suit
Powdered sugar to suit

Line a pie pan with a good crust. Put in a layer of fresh raspberries. Sprinkle with powdered sugar. Put in another layer of raspberries. Again sprinkle with powdered sugar. Continue doing this until pie shell is full. Cover with top crust but do not pinch down edges. Bake immediately at 425 degrees for 10 minutes. Then reduce heat to 350 degrees and bake 25 to 35 minutes longer. While pie is baking, start the following:

½ cup milk	2 egg whites
½ cup cream	1 tbls sugar
½ tsp cornstarch wet in cold milk	

Blend milk and cream in saucepan. Bring to boil. Then beat egg whites with sugar until stiff. Stir this into boiling milk and cream. Add cornstarch last to thicken. Boil three minutes. Take off stove and set aside to cool.

Remove pie from oven when done. Lift off top crust. When above mixture is cold, pour over raspberries in pie. Place top crust back on. Set pie aside to cool. Sprinkle sugar over the top crust before serving.

** ** ** ** **

This old recipe was a favorite of Carl Schurz (1829-1906), a young *Bible* believing Christian who fled Germany and immigrated to the United States in 1852. He became a close friend of Abraham Lincoln, sometimes prayed with him, and was one of his first supporters for the Presidency. Schurz was Lincoln's ambassador to Spain in 1861 and was made a brigadier general in the Union army in June of 1862. He was in command of a division at Second Bull Run and later commanded German speaking troops at Chancellorsville and Gettysburg. No citizen ever understood his country better. This man gave us what is one of America's finest concepts of patriotism with these immortal words: *"My country right or wrong; if right to be kept right; if wrong to be set right."*

General Canby's Favorite Prune Pudding

1 cup flour	1 cup cooked prunes
3 tsp baking powder	1 cup dry bread crumbs
3/4 tsp salt	1 cup suet, ground
½ tsp cinnamon	1 cup sugar
½ tsp cloves	1 cup milk

3 eggs, well beaten

Sift together in a wooden mixing bowl the flour, baking powder, salt, cinnamon and cloves. Mash cooked prunes to a pulp by rubbing through a sieve. Combine in another bowl the prune pulp, dry breadcrumbs, ground suet, sugar, milk and beaten eggs. Mix thoroughly. Add this to dry ingredients and blend well. Fill well-greased 1 pound cans 2/3 full. Cover tightly. Steam 2 hours. Serve with sweetened whipped cream, *Lemon Molasses Pudding Sauce*, or *Maple Syrup Pudding Sauce* (See last page of this chapter for these recipes). Makes 8 servings.

** ** ** ** **

Major General Edward Sprigg Canby (1817-73) was in charge of the troops in New York City when draft riots broke out in 1863. On March 17, 1865, this outstanding Christian military leader commanded two Union columns moving toward Mobile, Alabama. On April 12, Canby's troops occupied Mobile. The war in this part of the Confederacy was ended when Canby accepted the surrender of Lieutenant General Richard Taylor on May 4. This Union military leader graduated from West Point in 1839. He was murdered by Modoc Indians in the Pacific Northwest during a parley.

Buttermilk Pie – A Jeb Stuart Favorite

2/3 cup sugar
2 tbls flour
½ tbls butter, melted
1 cup buttermilk

1/8 tsp salt
4 tbls lemon juice
2 egg yolks, slightly beaten
2 egg whites

2 tbls sugar

Combine 2/3 cup sugar, flour and melted butter in a wooden mixing bowl and stir together. Add buttermilk, salt, lemon juice and slightly beaten egg yolks. Blend thoroughly. Pour mixture into 8 inch pastry lined pie pan. Bake at 425 degrees for about 40 minutes or until inserted knife blade comes out clean. When pie is finished, put two egg whites and 2 tablespoons sugar in a small bowl and beat until fluffy. Cover with this meringue and bake at 325 degrees for 20 minutes longer.

** ** ** ** **

Major General James Ewell Brown "Jeb" Stuart (1833-64) wrote to Jefferson Davis in January of 1861 and requested a commission in the "Army of the South." He was mortally wounded and his command defeated on May 11, 1864, during a fierce battle at Yellow Tavern, just North of Richmond, Virginia. Stuart's death was a devastating blow to the Confederacy. This dashing young Christian officer was but 31 years old when he died. He never doubted that he was fighting for what he called *"the will of the Almighty."* Stuart was born on Laurel Hill plantation in Patrick County, Virginia, and graduated from West Point in1854. He fast gained a reputation as a brilliant military strategist and a dashing leader. His daring wartime exploits made J.E.B. Stuart one of the legendary heroes of the Confederacy.

Vinegar Pie? Yes! The Longstreet Family
Enjoyed it Often

1 pastry shell, baked

3 egg yolks, beaten	2 cups water, boiling
1 cup sugar	¼ cup vinegar
3 tbls flour	1 tsp lemon juice
1/3 tsp salt	3 egg whites

3 tbls sugar

Put egg yolks in wooden mixing bowl and beat until thick. Add sugar, flour and salt. Mix thoroughly. Slowly add boiling water while stirring constantly. Stir in vinegar. Continue stirring mixture until thick and smooth. Lastly stir in lemon juice. Pour into previously baked pastry shell. Set aside while beating egg whites and 3 tablespoons sugar in separate bowl until stiff. Cover pie with this meringue. Bake at 325 degrees for 20 minutes.

** ** ** ** **

Lieutenant General James Longstreet (1821-1904) graduated near the bottom of his class at West Point in 1838. Others to be found in his class included such future distinguished Civil War Leaders as W.T. Sherman and

89

Ulysses S. Grant. Longstreet, a Christian, was accidentally shot by one of his own soldiers while on a reconnaissance mission in May of 1864. It happened just after he had led a successful attack against enemy Union forces. Longstreet did recover, however, but he was unable to return to duty for nearly 6 months. He commanded Confederate troops at such places as the First Battle of Bull Run, Williamsburg, Seven Pines and Fredericksburg. General Robert E. Lee considered Longstreet to be his most reliable commander and affectionately dubbed him his "Old War Horse." Regarding his personal beliefs, General Longstreet was clear in this regard when he declared: *"I am pleased to say: I believe in God, the Father, and his only begotten Son, Jesus Christ, our Lord. It is my custom to read one or more chapters of my Bible daily for comfort, guidance, and instruction."*

The Hood Family Pudding Sauces

Maple Syrup Pudding Sauce

2 egg whites	1 tsp lemon juice
½ cup cream	¾ cup maple syrup

¼ cup water

Put the egg whites, cream and lemon juice in a wooden mixing bowl. Beat this mixture until whites are stiff. Now put maple syrup and water in a saucepan and bring to a boil while continuously stirring. Continue boiling until the liquid will spin to a thread-like consistency. Immediately pour this into stiffly beaten egg white mixture while beating constantly with eggbeater.

Lemon Molasses Pudding Sauce

1-cup molasses	2 tbls butter

1/3 cup lemon juice

Put molasses in saucepan and bring to boil while stirring constantly. Add butter and let mixture boil for 1 minute. Lastly take off stove and stir in lemon juice. Blend thoroughly and serve over pudding. This is an excellent sauce for any steamed fruit pudding.

** ** ** ** **

John Bell Hood (1831-79) graduated from West Point in 1853 near the bottom of his class. But this apparently had no bearing on this young Christian officer's later success as an outstanding military man. He initially saw service on the frontier in California and Texas where he quickly became a favorite of his commander, Robert E. Lee, another well-known Christian leader. Hood joined the Confederate cavalry in April of 1861 and fast became known as the "fighting general" who rode into battle strapped to his horse. This great soldier was an inspiration to his men and others all throughout the Civil War. "Hood's Brigade" became famous and was the unit that all others aspired to become more like. Sadly enough, this great warrior died in bed of yellow fever just after the terrible epidemic of 1878, and not on the battlefield as he no doubt would have chosen.

** ** ** ** **

9

Pickles, Relishes and Sauces from Many Years Ago

Mrs. Johnston's Secret Green Tomato Pickle Recipe

1 peck green tomatoes	2 quarts cider vinegar
4 medium-size onions	1 pound brown sugar
1 head cauliflower	1 pound sugar
4 green peppers	1 tbls cloves
1 bunch celery	1 tbls allspice
1 cup salt	1 tbls peppercorns

1 tbls mustard seed

Take the green tomatoes and onions and slice thin. Separate the cauliflower head into small flowerets. Remove seeds from green peppers and chop peppers into pieces. Separate celery stalks and dice. Now place vegetables in large kettle in layers. Sprinkle each layer lightly with salt. Cover and let stand overnight. In the morning, drain off liquid. Add 1quart cider vinegar and 2 quarts water. Bring to boil. Let simmer 15 minutes. Drain again. Add other quart cider vinegar, brown sugar and sugar. Tie cloves, allspice and peppercorns in cheesecloth bag and drop in kettle. Bring to boil once again. Let cook 15 minutes to thicken to a syrup. Dip into canning jars while mixture is hot. This recipe makes 5 quarts of delicious old-fashioned green tomato pickles.

** ** ** ** **

The mother of Brigadier General Joseph Eggleston Johnston (1807-91) always held devotions after the family finished their evening meal and prayed with her son nightly before he went to bed as a child. She often made Joseph these pickled green tomatoes when he was growing up. Johnston was a graduate of West Point and the son of a veteran of the Revolutionary War. He resigned his U. S. Army commission in April of 1861 to join the Confederate military. One of this man's claims to fame was that he had made a major and decisive contribution to the Confederate victory at the Battle of Bull Run on July 21, 1861. He was appointed to the rank of full general shortly thereafter. This man had an enviable reputation as a Civil War commander. He was one of the elite few who had never lost a battle.

Beet Relish as Made by the Davis Family

1 quart cooked beets, chopped fine	2 cups sugar
	2 tbls salt
1 small head cabbage, chopped fine	2 tsp mustard
	2 tsp celery seed
1 cup horseradish, grated	1 pint vinegar

Put chopped beets and chopped cabbage in a large pot and stir together until well mixed. Then add grated horseradish, salt, mustard, celery seed and vinegar. Blend everything well. Cover and let stand at least 24 hours before using. This relish will keep indefinitely. It may be bottled or kept in a covered stone crock.

** ** ** ** **

Jefferson Davis (1808-1889), President of the Confederacy, was arrested and imprisoned in Fortress Monroe at the end of the Civil War. He was manacled and treated harshly like a common criminal rather than as a widely admired and respected leader of a great cause. So hated and feared was this great Christian leader by President Andrew Johnson, that Johnson insisted Davis had committed crimes *"worse than murder."* He wanted Davis on the scaffold with a noose around his neck as did many of the more radical, hate filled Northern leaders. Fortunately, their wishes to have him hanged did not prevail. Nevertheless, Davis spent two years in prison without ever being tried for anything! All he was allowed to read was his *Bible* and his prayer book. But this Godly man prevailed and was finally released in May of 1867 after the controversy over his unjust imprisonment grew to international proportions.

Lieutenant Buford's (Loreta Janeta Velazquez) Favorite Cucumber Relish

12 cucumbers	1 pound brown sugar
2 quarts small onions	1 quart vinegar
3 red peppers	1-1/2 tsp white mustard seed
2 tbls salt	1 tsp tumeric

Slice cucumbers, onions and red peppers thinly. Remove seeds from peppers and throw away. Cut these vegetables into small pieces and put in cooking pot. Stir thoroughly. Sprinkle with salt. Set aside for 2 hours. Then drain. Add brown sugar, vinegar, white mustard seed and tumeric. Bring to boil. Let simmer 45 minutes or until vegetable pieces are tender. Spoon into sterilized jars and seal while hot.

** ** ** ** **

Lieutenant Harry Buford (Loreta Janeta Velazquez) (1842?-97), a spirited young woman, was born in Cuba to an aristocratic Catholic Spanish family. She came to the United States and was educated in New Orleans. Loreta met and fell in love with a young Confederate army officer. She was but 16 when they married in 1856, against the wishes of her family. A fiercely independent young lady, Loreta proceeded to join the army along with her husband while disguised as a man. She went under the fictitious name of Harry Buford. Loreta's husband was killed early in the war, but Loreta stayed in the army and fought on at First Bull Run and Fort Donelson. This heroic Christian patriot was eventually exposed as a woman in 1863. Yet, she continued to work for the Confederacy as a spy behind Union lines. She later wrote and published a book in 1876 called *The Woman in Battle.*

The Wurlitzer Family Spiced Currant Recipe

7 pounds currants   1 pint vinegar
5 pounds brown sugar   3 tbls cinnamon
                3 tbls cloves

Pick over currants carefully, wash, drain and remove stems. Put into large kettle. Add brown sugar and vinegar. Tie cinnamon and cloves in piece of muslin and toss into kettle. Bring to boil while continuously stirring mixture. Then let simmer for 1-1/2 hours while stirring now and then. Store in stone crock. Cover and keep in cool place. Rudolph Wurlitzer always enjoyed this as an accompaniment to cold meats.

** ** ** ** **

Rudolph Wurlitzer was an obscure bank clerk who started out with nothing but studiously saved his money and eventually founded the world famous Wurlitzer Company. Rudolph was a faithful church-going young man who had been brought up in a Godly home. His big break came when he obtained a huge contract from the Union army in 1861 to supply the military with trumpets and drums. His company would later become internationally known for its organs and juke boxes. Wurlitzer credited his business success as well as his success in life to his unwavering Christian beliefs.

Sweet Pepper Relish as Made by Mrs. Toombs

12 red peppers	1-1/2 pints vinegar
12 green peppers	2 cups sugar
12 medium onions	2 tbls salt

Slice open red peppers and green peppers. Remove and throw away seeds. Then mince peppers and put in large kettle. Take skin from onions. Now mince onions and toss into kettle with peppers. Add vinegar, sugar and salt. Blend everything well. Bring to boil and let simmer 10 minutes. Take from stove. Fill pint jars while hot and seal. Makes 4 pints.

** ** ** ** **

Brigadier General Robert Augustus Toombs (1810-85) was Georgia's turbulent Congressman from 1845 to 1853 and U.S. Senator from 1853 to 1861. A successful planter and lawyer, he briefly served as Confederate Secretary of State under Jefferson Davis from March to July of 1861 (unhappily though after having lost the Southern Presidency to Davis). General Toombs led the Army of Northern Virginia at Peninsula, Second Bull Run and Antietam. Strongly opposed to the Southern defensive strategy, the fiery Toombs resigned his commission in March of 1863 after being denied a promotion.

Corn Relish – A Howard Family Favorite

12 ears corn
2 large onions
1 red pepper
2 green peppers
1 small head cabbage

1-1/2 cups sugar
¼ cup salt
2 tbls mustard
¼ cup flour
½ tsp tumeric

4 cups vinegar

Cut corn from cob. Put into large wooden mixing bowl. Take skin off onions and throw away. Chop onions into small pieces. Add to mixing bowl with corn. Slice open red and green peppers. Discard seeds. Chop peppers and put into mixing bowl as well. Quarter cabbage, chop it up and put it into mixing bowl with other vegetables. Blend everything together nicely and set aside.

Blend sugar, salt, mustard, flour and tumeric in small bowl with 2 cups cold vinegar. Put other 2 cups into kettle and bring to boil. Mix these two together in kettle and again bring to boil. Stir constantly until slightly thickened. Now dump into kettle the chopped vegetables from wooden bowl previously set aside. Stir until nicely blended. Continue slowly cooking for 30 minutes. Pour into sterilized jars and seal while hot.

** ** ** ** **

Oliver Otis Howard (1830-1909) was a another great Union general who was a West Point graduate. He saw action at First Bull Run, in the Peninsular Campaign, Antietam, Fredericksburg, Chancellorsville and Gettysburg. This top flight Christian officer lost an arm and won the Congressional Medal of Honor for his heroism under fire at Fair Oaks. Yet, he still went on to fight at Lookout Mountain, Missionary Ridge, with General Sherman's Atlanta March to the Sea and the Carolinas Campaign. Howard ultimately became superintendent of West Point from 1880 to 1882 and retired as a major general. Howard University, which he founded, was named after him.

10

Favorite Beverages of Yesteryear

How Mrs. Thomas Lincoln Made Coffee For Abe

1 good size cup full ground coffee
1 quart boiling water
1 eggshell, crushed
1 egg, white only
½ cup cold water

Pour fresh ground cup of coffee into quart of boiling water in coffee boiler (cooking pot or saucepan). Add crushed eggshell and egg white. Stir well as it continues boiling for 15 minutes. Set off stove and add cold water to clear. Let stand a few minutes until grounds settle. Strain through muslin into coffeepot to get rid of grounds. Send to table immediately and serve while hot.

** ** ** ** **

"Abe was a moderate eater ... He sat down and ate what was sat before him, making no complaint; he seemed careless about this," declared Mrs. Thomas Lincoln, Abraham's stepmother. But she further reveals that her later to be famous stepson did seem to favor a good cup of hot coffee. And the above is exactly how she always made it for him. Mrs. Thomas Lincoln was a Godly woman who read her *Bible* nightly before retiring. Church services were something she would never consider passing up even in terrible weather. She remarked as to how she *"dearly loved the inspiration"* she always received while sitting in church.

Rhubarb Punch Favorites of Henry Ward Beecher

Beecher Family Rhubarb Punch

3 cups rhubarb juice   2 cups orange juice
6 cups water   1-1/2 cups grape juice
          ¾ cup sugar

Blend all the juices in large pitcher and stir until all sugar is dissolved. Add ice and serve cold.

The Beecher Family's Rhubarb-Cider Summer Cocktail

2 cups rhubarb juice   1 cup orange juice
2 cups cider   ¼ cup lemon juice
          Sugar to suit taste

Combine rhubarb juice, cider, orange juice and lemon juice in large pitcher. Stir in sugar to suit taste. Chill thoroughly and serve very cold. Makes 8 servings.

** ** ** ** **

Henry Ward Beecher (1813-87) was an outspoken opponent of slavery and the brother of Harriet Beecher Stowe, author of "Uncle Tom's Cabin." He was behind carbines being shipped to anti-slavery proponents in boxes labeled *"Bibles."* These rifles were called **"Beecher's Bibles."** Why? Because this well-known Protestant minister had publicly declared that there was *"more moral power in one of these instruments so far as the slaveholders were concerned than in 100 Bibles."*

Richard Gatling's Favorite Lemonade Drinks

Egg Lemonade Special

1 egg, beaten thoroughly   Juice of 1 lemon
3 tbls sugar   1 cup cold water

Put beaten egg in glass with sugar and lemon juice. Add water gradually and stir until sugar is completely dissolved. Serve cold.

Grape Juice Lemonade

Juice of 3 lemons   1/3 cup sugar
2 cups grape juice   1 quart ice water

Combine ingredients in large pitcher in order given. Stir thoroughly until sugar in completely dissolved. Chill for ½ hour. This quantity will make 6 water glasses or 18 punch glasses. Serve cold with thin slice of lemon with seeds removed in each glass.

** ** ** ** **

Richard Jordan Gatling (1818-1903), a North Carolina physician and a professed Christian, patented the revolving 6-barrel hand cranked Gatling machine-gun on November 4, 1862. But President Lincoln initially ignored this new weapon's military potential because Gatling was suspected of having Confederate sympathies. His new weapon could fire an astounding 250 rounds a minute. A few of these rapid-fire guns were first tried aboard Union ships during the Siege of Petersburg. Union General Benjamin Franklin Butler in Virginia later used twelve. The United States Army finally officially adopted the Gatling gun in 1866. Dr. Gatling sincerely believed that wars would cease to exist in the future because of the devastating weapon he had created.

The Wallace Family Special Concoctions for Special Social Events

Fruit Juice Jubilee Punch

3 cups sugar	1 cup raspberry juice
3 cups water	1 cup gooseberry juice
3 cups tea	Juice of 6 lemons
2 cups grape juice	Juice of 4 oranges
1 cup blackberry juice	5 cups ice water

Make syrup by blending sugar and water in large kettle. Bring to boil and let cook 10 minutes. Set aside to cool. Combine cooled syrup with tea. Add various fruit juices and ice water. Pour over cracked ice in punch bowl. Garnish with thin slices of oranges and lemons. Makes 30 servings.

Egg Nog Supreme

12 eggs	2 ounces rum
2 cups sugar	1 quart cream
1 quart whiskey	1 quart whipping cream

Break and separate eggs. Put egg whites in one wooden mixing bowl, yolks in another. Beat egg whites until they are stiff and fluffy. Beat egg yolks in other bowl until light while blending in the sugar. Next stir in the whiskey very slowly along with the rum. Then add the cream and stir lightly. Fold in the stiff egg whites. Lastly whip the whipping cream until it doubles its bulk. Add this to the eggnog mixture and serve immediately.

** ** ** ** **

Major General Lew Wallace (1827-1905), an Indiana native, served the Union with distinction in the Civil War at

Romney, Harpers Ferry, Fort Donelson and Shiloh. General Ulysses S. Grant commended him for saving Washington when it was about to be captured. This man, a Christian, served on the court martial board of President Lincoln's assassins. And he headed up the court martial of Captain Henry Wirz, commandant of Andersonville, the infamous Confederate prison in Georgia. Wirz, a physician, was unjustly tried and convicted for *"murder in violation of the laws and customs of war."* He went to the gallows on November 10, 1865, in the old Capitol Prison in Washington. Captain Wirz was the only military man executed for so called *"war crimes"* after the Civil War ended.

Mrs. Higginson's Special Orange Shake Drinks

Orange Cream Delight

¾ cup orange juice	1 egg yolk, well beaten
¼ cup cream	Few grains salt
	Sugar to suit taste

Combine orange juice, cream and beaten egg yolk in shaker. Add salt. Sweeten to suit taste. Shake well to blend all ingredients thoroughly. Pour over cracked ice in glass. Serve very cold. Makes 1 serving.

Orange-Buttermilk Special

2 oranges, juice only	1/3 cup cold water
1 lemon, juice only	Few grains salt
4 cups buttermilk	Sugar to suit taste

Combine orange juice, lemon juice, buttermilk and cold water in shaker. Add salt. Sweeten to suit taste. Shake well to blend all ingredients thoroughly. Pour over cracked ice in glass. Serve very cold. Makes 6 servings.

** ** ** ** **

Colonel Thomas Wentworth Storrow Higginson (1823-1910) of Boston, a former slave, gained a degree of fame during the Civil War as commander of the 54th Massachusetts Infantry. Regulations at the time were such that Union soldiers were supposed to be paid at 90-day intervals. When no paymaster appeared after seven months of duty, a Sergeant Walker became upset and ended up threatening an officer with bodily harm. He was court-martialed and sentenced *"to be shot to death with musketry."* Although Higginson agreed with Walker's legitimate grievance, he could do nothing to save the soldier's life. He wrote in his diary that the lack of pay *"impaired discipline, relaxed loyalty, and had begun to implant a feeling of sullen distrust"* among the black soldiers under his command. Higginson, a Christian, eventually died while in combat. He had formerly been pastor of the Free Church at Worcester.

Clara Barton's Delicious Mint Mixtures

Mintade Syrup

½ cup sugar   6 tbls mint leaves, chopped fine
½ cup water   2/3 cup lemon juice

Put sugar and water in saucepan and bring to boil. Let cook 5 minutes. Add chopped mint leaves and lemon juice. Stir and let stand overnight. Pour into jar. Cover and store in cool place until needed. Add as required to flavor iced tea, lemonade, or any combination of fruit punches or juice drinks.

Mint Lemonade

1 egg, well beaten   Mintade syrup to suit
½ lemon, juice only   Sugar to suit taste
½ cup cold water   Sprinkle of salt

Combine in a shaker the beaten egg, lemon juice and cold water. Add mintade syrup and sugar to suit taste. Lastly throw in a sprinkle of salt. Shake well. Pour over cracked ice in glass. Drink cold. Makes 1 serving.

** ** ** ** **

Clara Barton (1821-1912) was a well-known Christian philanthropist. She founded the *American Red Cross Society* or what we more commonly know today as the *Red Cross*. This brave woman became one of the first to volunteer her services to nurse the sick and wounded when the Civil War broke out in April of 1861. The Surgeon General, because of her valuable contribution to the war effort, granted Barton permission to expand her medical work to the front lines in July of 1862. Clara fast became known and loved by the fighting men as *"the angel of the battlefield."* After the Civil War ended, President Lincoln asked this great Christian lady to organize a search for soldiers who were listed as missing in action.

Mrs. Pender's Cardinal Party Punch

1 quart cranberries	1 cup orange juice
1 quart water	½ cup lemon juice
2 cups sugar	1 pint cider

Put cranberries in saucepan with water and bring to boil. Allow to simmer while stirring constantly until cranberries are soft. Strain through moistened cloth. Add sugar. Let simmer 6 minutes more, stirring constantly. Set aside to cool. Chill and then add orange juice, lemon juice and cider. Blend well. Dilute to taste with additional water. Serves about 30 people.

** ** ** ** **

Confederate General William Dorsey Pender (1834-63) was born in North Carolina. He graduated from West Point in 1854 but soon after resigned from the United States Army to join the Confederate Army as a captain. After seeing much action in such places as Seven Pines, Second Bull Run, Antietam, Fredericksburg and Chancellorsville, he became a major general by the time he was only 29 years old. Pender was mortally wounded at Gettysburg on the second day of fighting. He died on July 19. This young man was highly regarded by his peers as a top-flight officer and often compared to the great Stonewall Jackson.

11

Old Timey Corn Meal Specialties

Spider Corn Bread – A Favorite of Fightin' Joe Wheeler

2 eggs	1-1/3 cups corn meal
2 tbls sugar	1/3 cup flour
3 cups milk	1 tsp baking powder
1 tsp salt	2 tbls butter

Harshly beat eggs and sugar together in wooden mixing bowl. Lightly stir in 2 cups milk and salt. Gradually stir in corn meal, flour and baking powder. Make certain everything is well blended. Now melt butter in cast iron skillet. Turn skillet so as to grease sides. Pour creamy batter from mixing bowl into skillet. Smooth over top. Hold other cup of milk about 6 inches above skillet and slowly pour over top of batter in circular motion. Do not stir! Carefully place skillet in oven at 400 degrees. Bake for 30 minutes. When spider cake is done it will have streak of tasty custard running throughout. Serve hot with plenty of butter.

** ** ** ** **

Joseph Wheeler (1836-1906) was a Georgia man who went to West Point only to graduate near the bottom of his class. But what a soldier this man turned out to be! By 1864, this outstanding Christian military leader had become the senior Confederate cavalry officer and better known as "*fightin' Joe*." He saw action at Shiloh, Perryville, Stones River and Chattanooga. Wheeler also took part in the Knoxville and the Atlanta Campaigns and fought against Sherman during his famous March to the Sea. Wheeler had personally fought in more than 1,000 battles prior to his capture in May of 1865. He was, after the Civil War ended, an Alabama congressman for many years.

Skillet Baked Corn Bread – A Favorite of the Welles' Family

2 cups corn meal	1 tsp sugar
2 cups flour	2 tbls butter, melted
4 tsp baking powder	2 eggs
1 tsp salt	6 tbls whipping cream
1-1/2 cups water	

Sift together in a large wooden mixing bowl the corn meal, flour, baking powder, salt and sugar. In a separate bowl blend the melted butter, eggs, whipping cream and water. Combine the two mixtures. Beat thoroughly to a creamy batter. Then carefully pour batter into large, well-greased cast iron skillet. Bake very slowly at 275 degrees. Be sure to loosen the corn bread from the sides of the skillet as soon as a crust forms. Then turn over and bake other side as well. Makes enough delicious corn bread to feed 8 to 10 people.

** ** ** ** **

Gideon Welles (1802-78) was a *Bible* believing Christian man who enjoyed this corn bread dish often at family gatherings. He became President Lincoln's Secretary of the Navy in 1861 and served ably throughout the Civil War period. Welles became one of the President's most influential advisors and trusted cabinet members. This most influential man was almost solely responsible for developing a successful Federal shipbuilding program. He increased the Union naval fleet from 90 ships to 670 and from 9,000 to 57,000 men.

Mrs. Booth's Spoon Batter Bread

6 egg yolks	2 tsp baking powder
2 tsp sugar	3 cups milk
1 tsp salt	1 cup buttermilk
½ cup grits, boiled	6 egg whites, stiffly beaten
1 cup yellow corn meal	3 tbls butter

Put egg yolks in large wooden mixing bowl. Stir in sugar and salt. Beat until custard-like in consistency. Then blend in boiled grits. Sift together yellow corn meal and baking powder in a separate bowl. Add this, the milk and buttermilk to the beaten egg yolk mixture in mixing bowl. Lastly fold in stiffly beaten egg whites. Now melt butter in bottom of baking dish. Turn dish so as to butter sides as well. Pour in creamy batter. Bake at 350 degrees for about 30 minutes. This is a deliciously different old-time spoon bread. It bakes to the consistency of a souffle. Serve by scooping with large spoon from the baking dish. This recipe makes enough to feed 6 people.

** ** ** ** **

This is the spoon batter bread that the mother of infamous John Wilkes Booth (1839-65) made for her sons when they were children. The Booth boys were reared on a farm near Bel Air, Maryland, under the guidance of a strict Christian mother. John Wilkes Booth didn't get much of a formal education and started acting at the age of 17 in Baltimore's St. Charles Theater. He was considered to be one of America's brightest young up and coming actors. He was an outspoken sympathizer of the South from the beginning of the Civil War and zealously supported slavery. The Civil War, he believed, was simply a struggle between freedom and tyranny. So rabid was his thinking that his brother, Edwin, thought he was "*insane*" concerning this subject. Despite his early Christian home life, as we all now know, he grew up to become the notorious assassin of President Abraham Lincoln at Ford's Theater on April 14, 1865.

Johnny Cake As Eaten by Lincoln as A Young Man

1 cup yellow corn meal	Pinch of salt
½ cup sugar	1 cup milk
½ tsp baking soda	1 egg, well beaten
1 tsp cream of tartar	1 tbls molasses
	1 tbls butter, melted

Sift corn meal, sugar, baking soda, cream of tartar and salt together in a wooden mixing bowl. Then add milk, beaten egg, molasses and melted butter. Beat thoroughly until creamy and smooth. Pour batter into shallow greased baking pan. Bake at 375 for 30 minutes. Serve while hot.

** ** ** ** **

Mrs. Jack Armstrong of New Salem on the Sangamon River knew Abraham Lincoln well. She was a woman who often fed him in her home in 1831 while Lincoln worked as a log splitter and lived in the village. She stated that the future President was a man of simple culinary tastes. This is the Johnny Cake Mrs. Armstrong prepared for Mr. Lincoln. Mrs. Armstrong was a good God-fearing woman who always asked Lincoln to pass the blessing before they began eating a meal at her table. And she always had devotions after the evening meal. This woman noted that *"Mr. Lincoln never left my table until this was finished. He seemed to never be in a hurry. He was a sincere Godly man above all else."*

Steaming Breads Mrs. Johnson's Way

Steamed breads were made, according to Mrs. Johnson, in a mold, which was nothing more than a lard pail, or any kind of can with a tight fitting cover. The inside of the pail or can must first be thoroughly greased inside. Then it is to be filled 2/3 full with the bread mixture. Lastly, the can is set in a kettle with enough boiling water to reach half way to the top of the can.

Andrew Johnson's Favorite Steamed Corn Meal-Oatmeal Bread

1-1/2 cups corn meal	¼ tsp baking soda
1-1/2 cups rolled oats	3 tbls molasses
1-1/2 tsp salt	1-1/2 cups milk
2 tbls baking powder	1 egg, well beaten
2 tbls butter, melted	

Mix together in a large wooden mixing bowl the corn meal, rolled oats, salt, baking powder and baking soda. In a separate bowl beat together the molasses, milk frothy beaten egg and melted butter. Then combine the two mixtures. Beat thoroughly to a creamy batter. Turn batter into well-greased mold and cover tightly. Steam for 2 hours.

** ** ** ** **

Andrew Johnson (1808-1875) became Lincoln's running mate in 1864 and succeeded to the Presidency when Lincoln was assassinated. His wife, Eliza, whom he had married when he was 18 in 1827, taught him to read. Not one wanting to severely punish the Southern States after the Civil War, he vetoed the Reconstruction Act of 1867. But hostile Radical Republicans in congress overrode him. Johnson made many enemies when he tried to continue Lincoln's more moderate Southern reconstruction policies. They made an attempt to impeach this basically good man and failed by a single vote. Johnson was thereafter unable to moderate the harshness of the punishment meted out by the congressional hate mongers. Johnson was basically a decent Christian man who proclaimed: *"I do believe in Almighty God. And I also believe in the Bible."*

Bacon Corn Bread – A Favorite of General Nathan Evans

6 slices bacon	1 cup flour
1 egg, well beaten	3 tsp baking powder
1 cup milk	½ tsp salt

1 cup white corn meal

Fry bacon slices until crisp. Then chop into small pieces and set aside to cool. When cool, combine bacon pieces, beaten egg and milk in wooden mixing bowl. Sift together flour, baking powder and salt into same bowl with other ingredients. Lastly stir in corn meal and blend everything thoroughly. Grease shallow baking pan and pour in batter. Use a muffin tin if you like. Fill only about 2/3 full. Bake at 450 degrees for about 15 minutes. Makes 10 servings **NOTE**: *In the old South, especially Virginia, corn bread was made only with white, stoneground meal. And sugar was seldom used in corn bread recipes.*

** ** ** ** **

General Nathan George Evans (1824-68) of South Carolina was an outstanding Confederate cavalry officer. This man played an important role in the victorious battle of First Bull Run. Evans was later was awarded a gold medal and the formal thanks of the Confederate congress for his leadership role at Balls Bluff. But in 1863, this West Point graduate's career did a down turn. He was tried for disobedience and drunkenness. Although acquitted of all charges, his reputation was ruined and he was relieved of his command. Eventually returning to do battle again in 1864, Evans unceremoniously fell off his horse and was seriously injured. Although in and out of controversy, Evans proclaimed himself a Christian. He said this: ***"I believe in the Bible. I believe in God. I accept Jesus Christ as the Son of God. What is more important to believe in?"***

Hominy Corn Bread – A Reynolds' Family Specialty

1 cup hominy   1 cup milk
1 tbls shortening, melted ½ cup corn meal
2 eggs, well beaten   ½ tsp salt
1 tsp baking powder

Blend the hominy, melted shortening, beaten eggs and milk in a wooden mixing bowl. Stir in corn meal, salt and baking powder. Set this aside while greasing large baking pan. Now pour batter into pan. Bake at 425 degrees for 35 minutes or until a rich golden brown. Serves 6 people.

** ** ** ** **

Alexander Reynolds (1817-76) graduated from West Point in 1838 and fought in the Seminole War until 1855. He was then discharged from the army after being accused of serious *"account discrepancies."* Later reinstated, he was kicked out once again after going AWOL to join the Confederate forces. Reynolds became a general and commanded a brigade at Vicksburg, Chattanooga and Atlanta. After the Civil War ended, Reynolds left the country in 1869 and joined the Egyptian army. Quite successful, he became its Chief of Staff in 1875. Was General Reynolds a Christian? His words speak for themselves: *"I often get on my knees and pray to the Almighty. I talk to God often. I know Jesus is my Saviour and this means everything to me."*

12

Bread and Rolls from Another Era

The Henry Alexander Wise Family Recipe for Quick Rising Gluten Bread

2 cups water, boiling	1 tsp salt
2 cups milk	1 egg, well beaten
1 tsp butter	¼ yeast cake
Gluten flour to suit	

This unique gluten flour recipe is very old and comes from a handwritten recipe book. It was handed down over the years and is quite easy to follow. Here is exactly how it was originally written:

"Pour a pint of boiling water into a pint of milk; add a teaspoonful of butter and a teaspoonful of salt. Let it stand until it is lukewarm; then add a well-beaten egg, a quarter of a yeast cake dissolved, and enough gluten to make a soft batter. Cover and stand in a warm place to rise; then add enough gluten to make a soft dough, and knead it well. Form it into four loaves, and let rise again. Bake for one hour. Gluten bread requires less yeast and less time than ordinary bread."

** ** ** ** **

Henry Alexander Wise (1806-76) was Governor of Virginia from 1856 to 1860 when he ordered the execution of John Brown for his part in the raid on Harpers Ferry.

Wise, a Christian, initially opposed secession but later volunteered for Confederate military service. He was given a commission as a Brigadier General in May of 1861.. One of his sons was killed in action while fighting in Roanoke Island, North Carolina. General Wise fought at Petersburg and Richmond and he was with Robert E. Lee's army when Lee surrendered at Appomattox.

Battlefield Corkscrew Bread – A Favorite of Stonewall Jackson's Troops

8 cups flour	4 tbls lard
2 tbls baking powder	or
2 tsp salt	4 tbls meat drippings

1 cup milk
1 cup water

Sift together in a large mixing bowl or pot the flour, baking powder and salt. Rub lard or meat drippings into dry mixture. Gradually blend in milk and water. Mix thoroughly to a rather stiff dough that can be easily handled.

Have a good bed of coals ready. Place forked stick on both ends of coals to support stick used for cooking bread. Now take green stick an inch or so in diameter. Wind dough around it. Rest ends of green stick on the two forked sticks. Turn frequently until bread is brown and crisp on all sides. Then lift green stick holding bread off forked sticks. Slide bread off and it is ready to eat. This recipe makes enough bread to feed 6 to 8 people.

** ** ** ** **

General Thomas Jonathan "Stonewall" Jackson (1824-63) was only 39 when he died. This great Confederate leader was on a reconnaissance mission at dusk when one of his own men accidentally shot him. He passed away 8 days later. Jackson's loss was a devastating blow to the Confederacy. General Robert E. Lee wrote: ***"I know not how to replace him."*** Approximately 8 months earlier, in September of 1862, Harpers Ferry surrendered to General Jackson. He stopped his mount in front of the 9th Vermont, took off his hat, and quietly said: ***"Boys, don't feel bad. You couldn't help it. It was just as God willed it."*** Stonewall Jackson was General Robert E. Lee's most trusted corps commander in the Army of Northern Virginia. General Jackson stopped to say this prayer on the battlefield in Manassas: ***"Oh God, let this horrible war quickly come to an end that we may all return home and engage in the only work that is worthwhile – and that is the salvation of men."***

The Greenbow Family Homemade Rolls

1-1/2 cups flour	1-1/2 cups potatoes, mashed
½ tsp salt	2 tbls butter, melted
3 tsp baking powder	2 eggs, well beaten

Sift together the flour, salt and baking powder in wooden mixing bowl. Stir in mashed potatoes. Moisten with melted butter and well-beaten eggs. Work lightly with hands to form smooth dough. Turn onto slightly floured board. Roll out ½ inch thick. Cut into rounds with upside down drinking glass. Brush each roll with melted shortening. Fold over. Place on greased baking sheet. Brush over with egg wash (see below for recipe). Bake at 375 degrees for 15 to 18 minutes.

Egg Wash for Glazing Rolls

1 egg yolk	½ cup cream

Beat egg yolk in small bowl. Add cream and blend thoroughly. Coat surface of each roll with this mixture using soft pastry brush.

** ** ** ** **

Rose O'Neal Greenbow (1815-64) was the wife of a prominent Christian doctor in Maryland. Not only was this woman a highly connected hostess on the Washington political scene, but she was an undercover Confederate spy as well. She gave General P.G.T. Beauregard the battle plans drawn up by Union General Irvin McDowell for First Bull Run. Subsequently placed under house arrest, her home continued to be a beehive of Confederate intelligence. Finally put in jail in January of 1862, Rose still found ways to get important intelligence data to her Confederate friends. She was eventually tried and exiled to the South. Rose eventually went on a mission to England for the Confederacy, but while on her way back home she accidentally drowned.

General Miles Favorite Whole Wheat Bread

1 yeast cake	1-1/2 cups milk,
3 tbls brown sugar	scalded and cooled
1-1/2 cups water,	3 tbls butter, melted
lukewarm	7-1/2 cups whole wheat flour
	1 tsp salt

Put yeast and brown sugar in wooden mixing bowl with lukewarm water and let it dissolve. Then stir in milk and melted butter. Gradually blend in whole wheat flour. Lastly add salt. Knead thoroughly, being sure to keep dough soft and pliable. Then place dough in well-greased bowl. Cover and set aside in warm place to rise for about 2 hours. When doubled in bulk, turn dough out on lightly floured kneading board. Mold into loaves. Place in well-greased bread pans. Cover and set aside to rise again for about 1 hour, or until light. Bake at 350 degrees for about 20 to 25 minutes.

** ** ** ** **

General Nelson Appleton Miles (1839-1925) was a mere store clerk in Boston who spent hour upon hour praying for a chance at military greatness – and his prayers were finally answered!. He joined the Union army and fought at Chancellorsville, the Wilderness, Spotsylvania, Antietam and Petersburg. One of his many claims to fame was that he was in placed in charge of the detachment assigned the duty of guarding Confederate President Jefferson Davis at Fortress Monroe, Virginia. Miles later went on to become a famous Indian fighter on the Western frontier. He had the distinction of commanding the group that captured Geronimo in 1886. This man, starting out as a mere clerk in a store, went on to become the Commander-in Chief of the U.S. Army from 1895 to 1903. And who is to say that prayers are not answered?

The Sumner Family Recipe for Quick Graham Bread

½ cup brown sugar 1 cup flour
¾ cup cold water 1-1/3 tsp salt
½ cup shortening, melted 1 tsp baking soda
¾ cup milk 2 cups graham flour

Put brown sugar and cold water in wooden mixing bowl and stir until sugar is completely dissolved. Then stir in melted shortening and milk. Sift together into this mixture the flour, salt and baking soda. Then gradually add graham flour and blend thoroughly. Grease one loaf pan. Pour batter into pan and bake at 375 degrees for 1 hour.

** ** ** ** **

Charles Sumner (1811-74) of Massachusetts was a graduate of Harvard law school. He was a Senator from 1851 to 1874, an uncompromising abolitionist, and one of the fervent anti-South Radical Republicans. A fiery speaker, he insultingly denounced a prominent South Carolina Senator on the Senate floor in 1856. This resulted in his being severely beaten and seriously hurt in retaliation by Senator Preston Brooks of South Carolina. These injuries forced Sumner out of public life for almost the next 4 years. This profoundly influential orator held strong antislavery views and was a staunch advocate of emancipation and equal rights for blacks during and after the Civil War.

Special Laxative Bread Recipe From the Family of General Grant

2 cups whole wheat flour	2 cups oatmeal
2 cups flour	1 yeast cake

Warm water to suit

Put all of the above ingredients in a large pan and blend well. Add sufficient warm water to work into a smooth dough. Cover with a towel. Set aside to rise in a warm place. When risen, divide dough into 2 loaves. Mold them smoothly and quickly. Bake immediately at 350 degrees for 25 minutes. Eat a portion of this laxative bread once or twice a day.

** ** ** ** **

Ulysses Simpson Grant (1822-85) was a famed Union General and the 18th President of the United States from 1869 to 1877. Grant was a brilliant military tactician. He was a relentless warrior, constantly hammering away at the enemy. Never one to give up, Grant was ever persistent, a man of quiet determination and calm resolution. He had all the inherent qualities of a great military leader. Grant, a devout Christian, was never one to hide his thoughts on this subject. He once said: *"I believe in the Holy Scriptures, and whoso lives by them will be benefited thereby. Men may differ as to the interpretation, which is human, but the Scriptures are man's best guide."*

Gluten Roll Favorites of the MacArthur Family

1 yeast cake, crumbled	1 cup milk, scalded and cooled
1 tbls sugar	1 tbls butter, melted
1 cup water, lukewarm	3 cups gluten flour
	1 tsp salt

Put crumbled yeast cake, sugar and lukewarm water in wooden mixing bowl and stir until completely dissolved. Then stir in milk and melted butter. Gradually add gluten flour and blend thoroughly. Lastly add salt. Knead until dough is smooth and elastic. Place in well-greased bowl and cover. Set aside in warm place, free from drafts, to rise until light – about 2 hours. Then turn out of bowl onto lightly floured board. Break into rolls and mold nicely. Place on well-greased baking tins. Cover and let rise again until double in bulk – about 1 hour. Bake at 350 degrees for about 20 to 25 minutes.

** ** ** ** **

Arthur MacArthur (1845-1912) joined the Wisconsin Volunteers in August of 1862 and led his regiment in 9 major battles before he was 20 years old. He saw action at Perryville, Stones River, Missionary Ridge and in Atlanta. MacArthur won the **Medal of Honor** for his heroic exploits at Missionary Ridge. General Douglas MacArthur of World War 11 and Korean War fame was his son. Arthur MacArthur was brought up in a devout *Bible* believing Christian family and was a professed Christian himself.

13

Biscuits and Muffins – An Old Fashioned Delight

The Gresham Family's Peanut Muffin Treat

2 cups flour	1 egg, well beaten
3 tsp baking powder	2 tbls butter, melted
2 tsp salt	1 cup milk
4 tbls brown sugar	½ cup peanuts, chopped

Sift together flour, baking powder, salt and brown sugar in wooden mixing bowl. Blend beaten egg, melted butter and milk in separate bowl. Pour this mixture into dry ingredients and stir only until everything is nicely moistened. Lastly blend in chopped peanuts. Pour batter into greased muffin tins. Fill only 2/3 full. Bake at 425 degrees for 25 minutes.

** ** ** ** **

Walter Quinton Gresham (1832-95), an attorney, served credibly as a colonel with the 52nd Indiana Volunteers. Politically inclined, this devout Christian eventually became Postmaster General in 1882 and Secretary of the Treasury in 1884 during President Chester Arthur's administration. In 1888 he was a prominent candidate for the Republican nomination to the Presidency. President Grover Cleveland later appointed him as his Secretary of State. He held this office until May 28 when he died.

Squash Biscuits as Made by the Rosecrans Family

1 yeast cake   1 cup sugar
1 cup water, lukewarm   2 tbls butter, softened
2 cups squash   ½ tsp salt
                  Flour to suit

This is to be started before going to bed. Crumble yeast cake in lukewarm water and stir until completely dissolved. Set aside momentarily. Now rub squash through a sieve and put in wooden mixing bowl. Add sugar, softened butter and salt. Beat together until all are well blended. Add yeast and beat once again to blend. Sift flour. Add just enough to mixture in bowl to make stiff batter. Cover and leave in warm place over night. In the morning put into greased biscuit tins. Bake at 400 to 425 degrees for 15 minutes.

** ** ** ** **

William Starke Rosecrans (1819-98), a Christian, came from a family with outstanding credentials. He was the great grandson of another well known Christian leader in America, Stephen Hopkins, Colonial Governor of Rhode Island and a

Signer of the *Declaration of Independence*. Rosecrans graduated from West Point in 1842 with such later to become famous classmates as General James Longstreet and General Abner Doubleday, later to become credited with the founding of America's pastime -- baseball. When the Civil War broke out, Rosecrans became commanding officer of the 23rd Ohio Volunteer Infantry, which had among its members future Presidents Rutherford Hayes and William McKinley. Rosecrans soon became a Brigadier General in the Union army and won an early victory when he defeated General Robert E. Lee at Rich Mountain, Virginia. On October 24, 1882, he took command of the Army of the Cumberland. Rosecrans, fondly nicknamed "Old Rosie," was highly regarded as a military strategist by those who knew him best.

Mrs. Kilpatrick's Whole Wheat Biscuits

2 cups whole wheat flour	4 tbls sugar
1 tsp salt	4 tbls shortening, melted
4 tbls baking powder	¾ cup milk

Sit together the flour, salt, baking powder and sugar in a wooden mixing bowl. In a separate bowl add the melted shortening to the milk. Blend well. Stir this into the dry ingredients to moisten, making the dough so soft as to be almost sticky. Turn out onto a lightly floured board. Roll or pat out to ½ inch thick. Cut into biscuits with biscuit cutter or upside down water glass. Place on well greased baking sheet. Brush over with a little melted butter. Bake at 375 degrees for 15 to 18 minutes. Serve while hot.

** ** ** ** **

Hugh Judson Kilpatrick (1836-81) came off a farm in New Jersey and graduated from West Point in May of 1861. This young man wasted no time in joining a New York cavalry regiment and was appointed a lieutenant colonel. He was severely wounded in June of 1861 at Big Bethel. Kilpatrick was one of the most flamboyant cavalry officers in the Union army. His unit became known as *Kill Cavalry* after he led the notorious Kilpatrick-Dahlgren Raid on Richmond in 1864. General Sherman had this to say about him: *"I know Kilpatrick is a hell of a damned fool, but I want just that sort of man to command my cavalry."* Kilpatrick, a devout Bible believing Christian, was given command of General Sherman's mobile forces during the famed March to the Sea, the Carolinas Campaign and the Atlanta Campaign.

Corn Meal Muffins as Made by Gail Borden's Family

4 tbls shortening	4 tsp baking powder
4 tbls sugar	½ tsp salt
1 egg, well beaten	1 cup corn meal
1 cup flour	1-1/4 cups milk

Put the shortening and sugar in a wooden mixing bowl. Using a fork, cream these together until light. Stir in the beaten egg. Sift together the flour, baking powder and salt in a separate bowl. Then blend the corn meal. Slowly add this dry mixture, alternately with the milk, to the first mixture in the wooden bowl. Beat together thoroughly. Pour batter into well greased muffin tins. Fill each about 2/3 full. Bake at 375 degrees for about 25 minutes. Serve while hot.

** ** ** ** **

Gail Borden (1801-75) produced a lot of condensed milk in his factories during the Civil War. . A patent was issued for condensed milk in 1851. And in 1861, America's first milk condensing plant was built in New Jersey. The Union army purchased most of Borden's milk for use in field rations because of its long shelf life. Mr. Borden faced a rather unique problem during the Civil War. His son Lee joined the Confederate Army and proudly rode with the Texas cavalry. John Gail, his other son, decided to go in the other direction and fight for the Union. Borden attributed his success in life to his strong belief in God and to the Christian upbringing his mother provided him as a child.

General Benavides Favorite Ham Muffins

2 cups flour   1 egg, well beaten
4 tsp baking powder   1 cup milk
2/3 tsp salt   2 tbls butter, melted
                1 cup ham, minced

Sift together in a wooden mixing bowl the flour, baking powder and salt. Then blend in the beaten egg, milk and melted butter. Mix well until a nice smooth batter is made. Set aside and prepare well-greased muffin tins. Put in a generous tablespoon of batter for each muffin. Then add a portion of minced ham. Cover with more batter. Bake at 375 degrees for about 20 minutes. Serve hot.

** ** ** ** **

Brigadier General Santos Benavides was the God fearing Mexican leader who commanded the Texas cavalry. His group gained some degree of fame as *"The Confederacy on the Rio Grande."* That was the area of the country they protected. Benavides and his brave followers were the Hispanic defenders of Dixie. Benavides, a Catholic, read the *Bible* to his officers each and every evening before settling in for the night. Attendance was mandatory in order for a man to serve under his command.

Gilbert Van Camp's Favorite Sweet Potato Biscuits

¾ cup sweet potatoes, mashed	1-1/4 cups flour
	4 tsp baking powder
2/3 cup milk	1 tbls sugar
4 tbls butter, melted	1 tsp salt

Blend mashed sweet potatoes, milk and melted butter in wooden mixing bowl. Sift together flour, baking powder, sugar and salt in same bowl. Mix thoroughly to make soft dough. Turn out on floured board. Toss lightly until outside of dough appears smooth. Roll out to ½ inch thick. Cut with floured biscuit cutter or upside down drinking glass. Bake on greased baking tin at 450 degrees for about 15 minutes.

** ** ** ** **

Gilbert G. Van Camp, a grocer in Indianapolis, Indiana, was only 37 when a brilliant idea struck him. This former tinsmith created a new kind of canned food staple for Union Army troops to eat when out on the battlefield. Thus evolved what we know today as Van Camps Pork and Beans and the many other canned goods commonly found in our grocery stores. Van Camp credited all of his business success to his unwavering belief in God and in doing good for others whenever the opportunity arose.

Beaten Biscuits as Enjoyed by General John Bankhead Magruder

4 cups flour	1 tsp salt
1 tsp baking powder	1 tbls shortening
7/8 cup ice water	

Sift together the flour, baking powder and salt in a wooden mixing bowl. Cut in the shortening with a fork. Add ice water. Knead with hands until a smooth dough is obtained. Turn the dough out onto a board and pat with a rolling pin until it blisters. Keep folding dough together and patting with rolling pin as it spreads on board. This procedure usually takes about 20 minutes. When full of blisters, roll dough out to about ¼ inch thick. Cut into biscuits with biscuit cutters or an upside down water glass. Prick each biscuit with a fork. Place biscuits on baking sheet. Bake at 375 degrees for 15 minutes. Serve while hot with plenty of butter on the side or with gravy over them.

** ** ** ** **

General John Bankhead Magruder (1810-71) was one of the Confederacy's first most acclaimed military heroes. He became a celebrity throughout the South because if his significant victory at Big Bethel on June 10, 1861. An 1830 West Point graduate, Magruder resigned his U.S. Army commission in March of 1861 and became a colonel in the Confederate service. An incredibly good leader, he soon thereafter was promoted to brigadier and then to major general in a matter of months. When the Civil War ended, this proud and dedicated Christian defiantly refused to ask for a parole and instead went into exile in Mexico where he became a major general under Maximilian.

14

Cakes and Frosting as Made During the Civil War

Biscuit Shortcake – A Meade Family Favorite

2-1/2 cups flour	2 tbls sugar
4 tsp baking powder	5 tbls shortening
½ tsp salt	¾ cup milk

Sift together the flour, baking powder, salt and sugar in a wooden mixing bowl. Then cut in the shortening with a fork. Add milk and blend everything until smooth dough is obtained. Divide dough into two even portions and place on lightly floured board. Roll each portion out to 1/3 inch thick. Brush over both with melted butter or other shortening. Place one rolled piece on slightly greased baking sheet. Place other on top of the first. Bake at 425 degrees for about 20 minutes. Take from oven when done and separate layers. Spread first layer thickly with crushed, sweetened fruit. Replace top layer. Put more fruit over it. Serve with cream or a thin custard. This can also be made as individual shortcakes, if preferred, by cutting dough with biscuit cutter or over turned drinking glass before baking

** ** ** ** **

General George Gordon Meade (1815-72) entered West Point in 1831. He was shot in the hip at Glendale and saw action at Antietam, Fredericksburg and Chancellorsville. Meade replaced General Joe Hooker as Commander of the Army of the Potomac on June 28, 1863. He was the man who was instrumental in the devastating defeat of General Robert E. Lee at Gettysburg in July of 1863. This defeat is believed to have been the South's one most crucial loss of the Civil War. General Meade was a devout Christian as can be attested to by the words of his son: *"General Meade's religious principles were exhibited in his daily life, in his intercourse with his fellow men, and the Christian example he set. As far as his outward profession of belief was concerned, he was an active and attentive communicant in our church from an early day, and died in the triumphs of faith in the great Captain of his salvation."*

Mrs. Lee's Best Coffee Nut Sponge Cake

2 eggs	1 tsp vanilla extract
1 cup sugar	1-1/2 cups flour
½ cup strong coffee, hot	2 tsp baking powder
3/4 cup pecans, chopped fine	

Beat eggs in wooden mixing bowl until light and thick. Gradually add sugar while beating constantly until sugar is dissolved. Add hot coffee slowly, stirring well. Then stir in vanilla extract. Sift together directly into this mixture the flour, and baking powder. Lastly add finely chopped pecans. Stir everything together lightly, just enough to blend nicely. Pour batter into ungreased tube pan. Bake at 325 degrees for about 1 hour. Makes one tasty 8-inch sponge cake.

** ** ** ** **

General Fitzhugh Lee (1835-1905) was the Virginia born nephew of the great Civil War General Robert E. Lee. He graduated from West Point with the class 1856 and initially served on the Western frontier. Fitzhugh, a devout Christian from a solid Christian family, initially led a Confederate cavalry brigade under the famed Major J.E.B. Stuart at Antietam, Gettysburg and Chancellorsville. He later commanded the cavalry for his uncle, General Robert E. Lee, during the final campaign of the Civil War – the retreat to Appomattox. Fitzhugh later took a command post in the U.S. Army in 1898 during the Spanish American War and served his country in Cuba.

The Davis Family Favorite Holiday Fruit Cake

2 cups butter	1 tsp cinnamon
2 cups sugar	4 cups flour
6 egg yolks, well beaten	¾ cup citron, chopped
1 tsp baking soda	and floured
2 cups sour cream	¾ cup cherries, chopped
1 tbls rose water	and floured
1 nutmeg, grated	6 egg whites, stiffly beaten

Put the butter and sugar together in a wooden mixing bowl and cream with a fork. Stir in beaten egg yolks. Dissolve baking soda in a little hot water in separate bowl. Stir this into the sour cream. Now add sour cream, rose water, nutmeg and cinnamon to the mixture in wooden mixing bowl. Next, gradually add flour and blend thoroughly. Work in the floured citron and cherries. Lastly, fold in the stiffly beaten egg whites. Line loaf pans with well-buttered paper. Pour batter into these pans. Bake at 275 degrees for at least 2 hours. **NOTE:** *This, according to Varina Davis, "is a wonderful fruit cake," and she was known to have made it often for her husband.*

** ** ** ** **

Jefferson Davis (1808-1889), President of the Confederate States of America. His father had fought in the Revolutionary War as the leader of an irregular cavalry troop. Davis, a strong *Bible* believing Christian, graduated from West Point in 1828, one year ahead of Robert E. Lee. In 1835, he married the daughter of his garrison commander, future President Zachary Taylor, against her father's wishes. Resigning because of her father's disapproval, they moved to Brierfield, a small Mississippi plantation. She died months later of fever. He again married a decade later, this time to Varina Howell, a prominent Mississippi planter's daughter, who was to become the First Lady of the Confederacy. He got into politics as a congressman, then a senator, and made a name for himself when he commanded a regiment of Mississippi volunteers in the successful Battle of Buena Vista in 1847.

Sponge Cake Chantilly as Made by Mrs. Wallace

3 egg yolks	1-1/2 cups flour
1 cup sugar	2 tsp baking powder
½ cup milk	½ tsp salt
1 tsp vanilla extract	4 tbls butter, melted

3 egg whites, beaten until stiff

Put egg yolks in wooden mixing bowl with sugar. Beat until thick and yellow. Stir in milk and vanilla extract. Sift together the flour, baking powder and salt. Gradually stir this into mixture in wooden bowl. Add melted butter. Lastly fold in stiffly beaten egg whites. Grease and flour 2 large cake pans. Turn batter mixture into these pans. Bake at 350 degrees for 15 to 20 minutes. Set aside to cool. Then put chocolate pudding between the layers. Cover top layer with Chantilly Cream (see below).

Mrs. Wallace's Chantilly Cream

1 egg, white only   2 tbls currant or quince jelly

Place egg white and jelly together in large wooden mixing bowl. Beat until stiff, like whipped cream. Pile on top of cake and sprinkle thickly with coconut.

** ** ** ** **

Union General Lewis Wallace (1827-1905) of Indiana successfully thwarted a Confederate cavalry attack on Washington led by General Jubal Anderson Early on July 9, 1864. General Grant commended this outstanding Christian military leader for saving the city. Wallace had also been instrumental in stopping Cincinnati from falling into Confederate hands in 1863. Highly regarded by all who knew him, Wallace fought at Romney and Harpers Ferry.

He bravely led divisions at Fort Donelson and Shiloh. General Wallace earned rapid promotions and became a Brigadier General in March of 1863. This man also handled the important administrative work necessary in the court martial of President Lincoln's assassins and that of Henry Wirz, commandant of the notorious Andersonville Prison.

Angel Cake as Made by General Weisiger's Mother

7 egg whites	¾ cup pastry flour
¾ tsp cream of tartar	1-1/2 tsp baking powder
1 cup sugar	Few grains salt

1 tsp vanilla extract

Put egg whites in wooden mixing bowl. Beat harshly with wire beater until the whites foam. Add cream of tartar. Continue beating until whites stiffen. Gradually add sugar by folding into stiff egg whites with a spatula. Then proceed to sift together four times the pastry flour, baking powder and salt in a separate bowl. Fold these dry ingredients into the stiff egg whites. Lastly stir in vanilla. Bake in well-greased tube pan at 350 degrees for from 45 to 60 minutes.

** ** ** ** **

Brigadier General David Adams Weisiger (?-1899), a more or less forgotten man in history today, was the epitome of what a fighting man should be. He started out by serving in the Mexican War and later served as a colonel in the Virginia Militia. His Confederate led forces seized the Norfolk Navy Yard. Never one to avoid a good fight, Weisiger proudly fought for the Confederacy at Seven Pines, Second Bull Run, Petersburg, the Wilderness and innumerable other places during the Civil War. He was wounded for the first time at Second Bull Run. But his unbelievable courage showed through best at Appomattox. There this man was not only wounded three times, but two horses were shot out from under him in the heat of battle before he was finally forced to surrender. Weisiger, a Christian, feared nothing. He often told others that he truly believed he was protected by the hand of God in every battle throughout the war.

Three Layer Cake – A Hooker Family Special

1-1/2 cups sugar	1 tsp baking powder
1 cup butter, softened	½ tsp salt
3 eggs	½ tsp cloves
1-1/4 cups raspberry jam	1 tsp cinnamon
3 cups flour, sifted	½ tsp nutmeg
½ tsp baking soda	1 cup buttermilk

Put sugar in large wooden mixing bowl. Add softened butter. Beat together until light and creamy. Add eggs to this, one at a time, and beat thoroughly. Lastly, beat in raspberry jam. Set bowl aside temporarily. Using separate mixing bowl, sift together flour, baking soda, baking powder, salt, cloves, cinnamon and nutmeg. Add these dry ingredients, in three parts, alternately, with buttermilk to creamy mixture in wooden mixing bowl. Beat thoroughly after each part is added. Butter three round 9 inch cake pans. Line each with buttered and lightly floured paper. Pour equal amounts of batter in each pan. Bake at 350 degrees for 30 to 40 minutes or until toothpick inserted in center of cake comes out clean. Then remove pans from oven and set on wire racks for 10 minutes to cool. Turn cakes out and set aside until cooled. When completely cold, spread each layer with ***Boiled White Frosting*** (see recipe below). Stack frosted layers on each other and cover entire cake with same frosting.

Mrs. Hooker's Boiled White Frosting

1 cup, sugar	1 egg white
¼ cup hot water	Pinch cream of tartar
	Lemon juice to suit

Put sugar and hot water in sauce pan and bring to boil. Continue boiling until it strings. Don't stir. Meanwhile, put egg white in wooden mixing bowl. Beat until stiff. Then slowly pour sugar-water mixture into this and blend. Add cream of tartar. Beat thoroughly. Lastly, flavor to suit taste with lemon juice. Spread generously between layers and over cake as soon as it's ready.

NOTE OF HISTORICAL INTEREST:

When cakes like this were made in the Old South, many a housewife would stir a coin into the dough before baking. The family member finding the coin in his or her piece of cake was said to be going to have some sort of unexpected good luck. If the cake were served at a wedding, any single young woman finding the coin in her piece of cake was believed to be destined to be the next to be married.

** ** ** ** **

Major General Joseph Hooker (1814-79) graduated from West Point in the class of 1837 which included future Civil War generals Braxton Bragg, Jubal Early and John Sedgwick. Hooker was a tall, handsome and outspoken Christian who often stepped on the toes of his senior officers with his biting criticism. A boastful fellow, he once said: **"May God have mercy on General Lee, for I will have none."** He was subsequently soundly defeated by General Robert E. Lee at Chancellorsville in May of 1863. Hooker, never without his *Bible*, later went on to defeat Confederate General Braxton Bragg at the Battle of Lookout Mountain in Chattanooga, Tennessee, on November 24 of that same year. He was aptly called **"Fightin' Joe"** as a result of his many daring exploits on the battlefield during the Civil War.

15

Cookies to be Fondly Remembered

John Charles Fremont's Favorite Brown Sugar Cookies

¼ cup butter	1 cup flour
½ cup brown sugar	1 tsp baking powder
2 egg yolks, beaten	½ tsp salt
2 egg whites, beaten	¾ cup nuts, chopped
1/3 cup milk	Raisins to suit

Cream butter and brown sugar in wooden mixing bowl. Add beaten egg yolk. Blend well. Then add beaten egg white. Again blend thoroughly. Stir in milk. Sift flour. Measure out 1 cup. Sift again with baking powder and salt into first mixture. Lastly add chopped nuts. Mix everything thoroughly. Drop batter by teaspoonfuls onto lightly greased baking sheet. Press one raisin into the center of each cookie. Bake at 400 degrees for about 15 minutes. Makes 15 cookies.

** ** ** ** **

John Charles Fremont (1813-90), well known explorer, political leader and general, was raised in a South Carolina Christian family. He used Kit Carson, the noted mountain man, as his guide on his historic trek West. This man was a Union general in command of the Department of the West in July 1861. His administration was found to be corrupt, reckless and flamboyant. He was finally removed from office due to his excessively harsh policies regarding slave owners. He was transferred to the Mountain Department in March of 1862 but was a total failure in the 1862 Shenandoah Valley Campaign. He was then relieved of his command when he refused to serve under General John Pope, an old adversary.

Abraham Lincoln Ate These Honey Cookies in 1831

2/3 cup shortening	5 cups flour
½ cup sugar	1 tsp baking soda
1 cup honey, strained	½ tsp salt
1 egg beaten	½ tsp nutmeg
½ cup sour milk	½ tsp cinnamon
	½ tsp cloves

Cream shortening and sugar in wooden mixing bowl. Add honey and blend thoroughly. Stir in the beaten egg and sour milk. Now sift together in separate bowl the flour, baking soda, salt, nutmeg, cinnamon and cloves. Combine these dry ingredients with liquids in wooden mixing bowl. Blend well. Set aside and let chill. When chilled, put dough on floured board. Roll out to ¼ inch thick. Cut out cookies with cookie cutter or upside down drinking glass. Put cookies on greased baking tins and bake at 350 degrees for about 10 minutes. Makes about 4 dozen 2-1/2 – inch cookies.

** ** ** ** **

Abraham Lincoln moved in 1831 to New Salem, a small town on the Sangamon River where he worked as a rail-splitter. He boarded at Rutledge Tavern where he usually ate bacon, eggs and corn bread or scrapple for breakfast. He was known to have a special affinity for honey. A honey cookie, served to Abe by the beautiful Anne Rutledge who worked there as a waitress, was prepared exactly as shown above. Lincoln was without question a devoted Christian who prayed sincerely and regularly. He said this regarding the *Bible*: ***"In regard to this Great Book, I have but this to say, I believe the Bible is the best gift God has given to man. All the good Saviour gave to the world was communicated through this book."***

Molasses Cookies as Made by Mrs. Stanton

1 cup butter	1 tsp salt
1 cup molasses	1 tsp baking soda
1 cup brown sugar,	1 tsp cinnamon
firmly packed	2 tsp ginger
1 egg, well beaten	¼ tsp nutmeg
4 cups flour	½ tsp cloves

Combine butter, molasses and brown sugar in saucepan. Blend together and bring to boil over low heat. Let boil 2 minutes. Remove sauce pan from heat and let cool to lukewarm. Add beaten egg and mix thoroughly. Sift together the flour, salt, baking soda, cinnamon, ginger, nutmeg and cloves. Add to mixture in saucepan and blend well. Dump out onto lightly floured board. Form into 4 rolls 1-1/2 inches in diameter. Wrap each in buttered paper and chill overnight or longer. When ready, slice thin. Grease baking sheets. Place each slice on baking sheet 1 inch apart. Bake at 350 degrees for 10 to 15 minutes. Makes 10 dozen 2 inch cookies.

** ** ** ** **

Edwin McMasters Stanton (1814-69) was President Lincoln's Secretary of War after January of 1862. This man was an outstanding executive who completely reorganized the military and was able to root out corruption. Stanton, a professed Christian, was nevertheless widely disliked because of his abrasive personality. But he certainly was an honest man and one who got things done. He had this to say about the reaper invented by Cyrus McCormick*: "Without McCormick's invention, I feel the North could not win and that the Union would be dismembered."* Sadly enough, this great leader died just four days after he had been confirmed as a United States Supreme Court Justice.

Caraway Cookies as Eaten by General Burnside

1 cup butter	¼ tsp baking soda
1 cup sugar	¼ tsp salt
2 eggs, well beaten	½ tsp ginger
1 tbls milk	2 tbls orange rind, grated
1 cup flour	1 tbls caraway seeds

Cream the butter and sugar in wooden mixing bowl. Stir in beaten eggs and milk. Sift flour and measure out 1 cup. Then again sift with baking soda, salt and ginger. Add this to first mixture. Stir in grated orange ring and caraway seeds. Add sufficient flour to form soft dough. Blend thoroughly. Set aside to chill overnight. In the morning, turn dough out on lightly floured board. Roll out into sheet ½ inch thick. Cut into cookies with cookie cutter or upside down water glass. Lightly grease baking sheets. Place cookies on sheet and bake at 400 degrees for 10 minutes. Makes about 75 cookies.

** ** ** ** **

Ambrose Everett Burnside (1824-81, Union general, graduated from West Point in 1847. A close friend of President Lincoln, Burnside's genial nature and natural ability to make friends in high places brought him fast advancement in military rank. In November of 1862, Lincoln placed his friend in command of the Army of the Potomac in place of General McClellan. Burnside protested, as he rightfully should have, that he wasn't qualified for such a huge responsibility. But, politics being as they are, he got the job anyway. Future events proved Burnside to be all too correct in his self-appraisal. Although a dedicated Christian, he was all too often a disaster militarily although he did do well on the battlefield in some instances. But this handsome six-foot fellow, with the flamboyant whiskers and fluffy sideburns, was a huge postwar success. He successfully served as president of two railroads and was the director of a steamship company. Burnside was elected governor of Rhode Island in 1886, 1887 and 1888. And he served as a Rhode Island Senator from 1875 until he died on September 13, 1881.

Mrs. Reynolds Made These Sugar Cookies for Her Husband, John

1 cup butter	3 eggs, beaten
2 cups sugar	3 tsp baking powder
6 tbls milk	5-1/2 cups flour
2 tsp vanilla extract	1 tsp salt

Cream butter in a wooden mixing bowl. Gradually add sugar and work together with a fork until a creamy mixture is obtained. Blend together milk, vanilla extract and beaten eggs in second bowl. In yet a third bowl, sift together baking powder, flour and salt. Then add these dry ingredients, alternately, with milk-egg mixture to butter-sugar mixture in first bowl. Blend everything well. Set aside to chill. When thoroughly chilled, put dough on lightly floured board. Roll out to about ¼ inch thick. Cut into cookies with floured cookie cutter or upside down water glass. Lightly grease baking tin and place cut cookies on them. Sprinkle with sugar. Bake at 375 degrees for 10 to 12 minutes. Makes 4 dozen 2 inch cookies.

** ** ** ** **

Major General John Fulton Reynolds (1820-63) was commandant of cadets at West Point at the time the Civil War broke out. He became a Brigadier General in 1861 and fought at such places as Mechanicsville, Gaine's Mill, Second Bull Run, Fredericksburg and Chancellorsville. He was captured in July of 1862 at White Oak Swamp during the Seven Days' Battles. Reynolds commanded the First Union Corps at Gettysburg. This man was a highly regarded officer and known as one of the Union's most capable military leaders. He once told his men before going into battle: *"Never deny the truth of the Bible. Never show disrespect to the Lord."* Reynolds was killed by a sniper early on in the Battle of Gettysburg.

Dutch Cinnamon Snaps As Made by the Ferrero Family

1 cup sugar	2 tsp warm water
1 cup butter	5-1/2 cups flour
1 cup molasses	1 tbls cinnamon
2 tsp baking soda	1 tbls ginger
	½ tsp salt

Put sugar in wooden mixing bowl with butter. Blend together until creamy. Add molasses and stir in well. Dissolve baking soda in the warm water. Add to mixture in bowl. Sift together 2 cups flour, cinnamon, ginger and salt in bowl with other ingredients. Blend everything well. Add enough of remaining flour to make a dough firm enough to roll. Turn dough out onto lightly floured board. Roll in sheet about 1/8 inch or less thick. Cut with floured cookie cutter or upside down water glass. Lightly grease baking sheets. Place cut dough on sheets. Bake at 350 to 375 degrees for 8 to 10 minutes. Makes about 200 2 inch cookies.

** ** ** ** **

Edward Ferrero (1831-99) was a Spanish immigrant, a New York dance instructor and militiaman who ultimately became a Union general. He was a devout Catholic who served under General Ambrose Burnside in North Carolina and saw action at Second Bull Run, Fredericksburg, Vicksburg and Knoxville. This man has a claim to fame (or notoriety) that most men wouldn't care to have. The shameful thing he is most vividly remembered for is what he did at Petersburg Crater. There he gave his black division an order to charge – and then he promptly abandoned them!

Old Fashioned Ginger Cookies as Mrs. Lee Made Them

½ cup butter, melted	4 tsp baking powder
1 cup molasses	¼ tsp baking soda
2 tbls warm water	¼ tsp salt
1 egg, well beaten	½ tsp ginger
3 cups flour	1-1/2 tsp cinnamon

Blend together in a wooden mixing bowl the melted butter, molasses and warm water. Stir in beaten egg. Sift together into this mixture the flour, baking powder, baking soda, salt, ginger and cinnamon. Blend everything thoroughly. Set aside and let stand 15 minutes. Meanwhile, lightly grease baking sheets. When ready, turn dough out on lightly floured board. Roll out to 1/8 inch thick. Cut with floured cookie cutter or upside down drinking glass. Place cut dough on greased baking sheets. Bake at 375 degrees for 10 to 12 minutes. Makes 9 dozen 2-inch cookies. **NOTE**: *These cookies keep for a long time if stored in a stone jar or crock. Their flavor improves with age.*

** ** ** ** **

General Robert E. Lee (1807-70) will always be looked upon as a hero to the Southern cause. He was the fourth child of Revolutionary War hero Henry "Lighthorse Harry" Lee. A brilliant young man, he graduated second in his class at West Point. He married Mary Custis, the granddaughter of George Washington and Martha Custis Washington. Lee was judged to be the most promising officer in the U.S. Army when the Civil War broke out. Lincoln offered him field command of the Union army but instead Lee resigned his commission when Virginia seceded from the Union. Lee was a man who lived his Christian faith. Regarding the *Bible*, he once told Chaplain John William Jones: ***"There are things in the old Book which I may not be able to explain, but I fully accept it as the infallible Word of God, and receive its teachings as inspired by the Holy Spirit."***

Index

ABOUT THE AUTHOR

Robert W. Pelton has been writing for more than 30 years on a great variety of historical and other subjects. He has traveled extensively throughout the world as a researcher and has published hundreds of feature articles and numerous books. Pelton lectures widely, has appeared on many television shows, been a guest on a large number of radio talk shows, and has at one time even hosted his own radio show.

With the unique biographical sketches found in his historical recipe books, he clearly shows how the hand of Providence influenced those who fought and died for their cause in the War Between the States or what is more popularly called the Civil War -- or by many Southerners, even today, the War of Northern Aggression.

Pelton has been in demand as a speaker to diverse groups all over the United States. Tom R. Murray of the Council of Conservative Citizens, after hearing him speak a number of times, offers this: "Mr. Pelton puts together rare combinations of intellectual energies as a writer and speaker that will captivate all levels of an audience. I feel that no one can involve an audience and deliver an important message better than Mr. Robert Pelton."

Pelton may be contacted for convention speaking engagements and for talks before other groups at:

Freedom & Liberty Foundation
P.O. Box 12619
Knoxville, Tn   37912-0619
Fax: 865-633-8398
e-mail: cookbooks@juno.com